24 GREAT walks in BARCELONA

WILEY

Wiley Publishing, Inc.

Series Editor: Donna Wood
Art Editor: Alison Fenton
Proofreader: Fiona Wild
Picture Researcher: Liz Stacey
Cartography provided by the Mapping Services
Department of AA Publishing
Image retouching and internal repro: Michael Moody
Production: Stephanie Allen

Edited, designed and produced by AA Publishing.
© Automobile Association Developments Limited 2009

Published by AA Publishing.

Published in the United States by
Wiley Publishing, Inc.
111 River Street, Hoboken, NJ 07030

Find us online at Frommers.com

Frommer's is a registered trademark of Arthur Frommer.
Used under license.

Mapping © MAIRDUMONT/Falk Verlag 2008

ISBN 978-0-4704-5373-5
A03625

A CIP catalogue record for this book is available from
the British Library.

The contents of this publication are believed correct
at the time of printing. Nevertheless, the publishers
cannot accept responsibility for errors or omissions,
or for changes in details given in this guide or for
the consequences of any reliance on the information
provided by the same. Assessments of attractions and
so forth are based upon the author's own experience
and, therefore, descriptions given in this guide necessarily
contain an element of subjective opinion which may not
reflect the publishers' opinion or dictate a reader's own
experiences on another occasion.

Colour reproduction by Keene Group, Andover
Printed in China by Leo Paper Group

OPPOSITE: PLAÇA D' ESPANYA AND AV. REINA MARIA CRISTINA

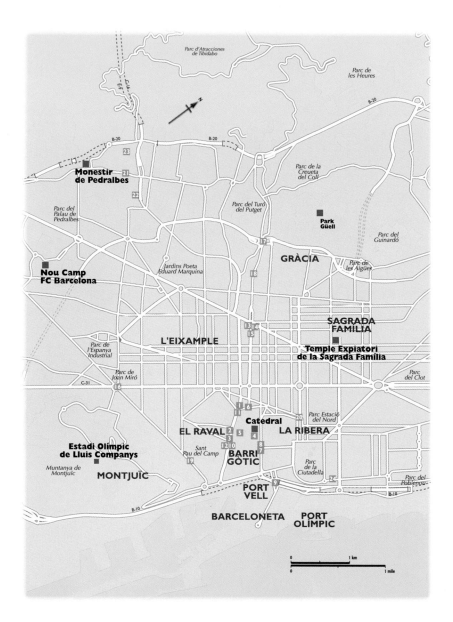

CONTENTS

Introduction

Barcelona is the perfect walking city. Narrow from top to bottom, it is neatly contained by the Collserola hills rising up behind the urban expanse. A high-speed hike from upper Barcelona to the port takes little more than an hour and a half.

A quick glance at a full-sized city map explains much of the city's history. The erratic jumble of streets at the centre bottom is the Ciutat Vella (Old City). Ciutat Vella is contained by traces of the 17th-century city walls finally torn down in 1860. The famous thoroughfare, the Rambla, divides the Old City in two. The left side, called the Raval (from the word *arrabal* for slum or outskirt), was originally outside the second set of 13th-century walls that ran down the right or east side of the Rambla. In the middle of the right side of the Ciutat Vella, following Carrer de la Palla, Carrer Banys Nous, Carrer Avinyó, and, on the north side, Carrer Sots-Tinent Navarro and Carrer Tapineria, the curve of the 1st-century Roman wall is clearly visible. The enclosed area, Roman Barcino, is often referred to as the *rovell de l'ou*, the yolk of the egg. In and around the Roman nucleus is the pedestrianized Gothic Quarter, while across Via Laietana is the Barri de la Ribera or waterfront district around the Santa Maria del Mar basilica. Further east is the fishermen's quarter, La Barceloneta, built on landfill in the mid-17th century.

The wide expanse of city blocks arranged in a grid square above Ciutat Vella is the Eixample or Expansion, designed in 1860 by urban planner Ildefons Cerdà after Barcelona finally got permission from Madrid to tear down its constricting city walls and expand into the hitherto empty no-man's land that is now the city's most elegant commercial and residential quarter. Curiously, the Eixample grid is neither numbered nor alphabetically ordered, so even longtime *barcelonins* can get lost there.

The formerly outlying villages of Sarrià, Sant Gervasi, Gràcia and Horta occupy the upper reaches of the city, but they can be reached in no more than 15 minutes by train from Plaça Catalunya and are worth exploring.

The city's three geometrical arteries – Paral.lel, Diagonal and Meridiana – were Cerdà's solution for rapid decongestion of the city.

Barcelona's public transport is cheap and easy to use. The trams are clean and quiet but, with one exception, don't serve areas of interest to visitors to the city. A T-10 multi-ride, multi-user, metro, bus, tramway, funicular ticket (about 8 Euros) allows travellers to use four different means of transport within 75 minutes for the price of one ride. Taxi fares seldom exceed 10 Euros, even late at night.

For anyone unlucky enough to have limited time in Barcelona, walks not to miss would be those based around the Rambla, followed by the Boqueria itinerary, the Gothic Quarter, La Ribera and Santa Maria del Mar, the Passeig de Gràcia-centred Eixample walk, and the Sagrada Família walk. The Top Three would be Rambla, Boqueria and Santa Maria del Mar, though a quick look at Gaudí's Sagrada Família and a turn through the Gothic Quarter between the Cathedral and Plaça Sant Jaume are difficult to imagine leaving without.

In all, Barcelona offers a vastly varied range of walking environments, from the Rambla's teeming runway to the Gothic Quarter's ghostly hush, the Raval's global fusion, Ribera-Born's twisting alleys, seafaring and laundry-festooned Barceloneta, the elegant Moderniste Eixample, Gràcia's young and Bohemian vibe, and the country village hillside of Sarrià-Sant Gervasi. Adding Pedralbes, Montjuïc, Park Güell and the Fòrum complex, that makes a dozen different Barcelonas to explore, each of them distinct and thick with secrets.

Bring a pair of sturdy walking shoes with you, as well as a raging appetite, and you cannot fail to enjoy your exploration of all these Barcelonas on foot, up close and personal, the way every beautiful city should be seen.

WHERE TO EAT

€	=	Inexpensive
€€	=	Moderate
€€€	=	Expensive

Rambla, River of Life

Barcelona's best-known boulevard is the Rambla. A continually self-renewing flow of humanity keeps the street in a constant state of flux.

The promenade that poet Federico García Lorca (1898-1936) called the only street he wished would never end, the rollicking Rambla is Barcelona's most famous thoroughfare. Its name originates from the Arabic *rmel* (sand), a reference to the sandy watercourse that once ran along the 13th-century walls on the east side of today's flood of humanity. The Rambla filled with water during spates of rain, but was usually flowing only with people: labourers, vendors, thieves, minstrels, prostitutes and grifters. From the Café Zurich, Barcelona's meeting point in Plaça Catalunya at the head of the Rambla, past the Betlem church at the intersection of Carrer del Carme and Carrer Portaferrissa to the Rambla de les Flors, where the flower stalls slow and tighten the human flow and fill the air with the heady musk of roses, there is much to explore. Forays into the streets off either side will reveal the hidden Romanesque church of Santa Anna, 1st-century Roman tombs, and a pot pourri of shops.

1 Start in front of the Café Zurich across from the head of the Rambla.

Begin with a coffee or a *caña* (draught beer) in the sun and a look inside this historic café, once the *cantina* of the Generalitat railroad and the oldest building in Barcelona's post-1860 expansion or *Eixample*. Across the street, notice the graceful Déesse sculpture by Josep Clarà (1878–1958) in the reflecting pool at the edge of Plaça de Catalunya. You will meet this voluptuous goddess again in the vestibule of the Barcelona Town Hall. The hard-edged block of marble competing for space is the Josep Maria Subirachs monument to Francesc Macià, president of the Generalitat de Catalunya from 1932 until his death in 1933. The Generalitat governed Catalonia during the Second Spanish Republic, the democratically elected government of Spain overthrown by Generalísimo Francisco Franco's 1936 military rebellion. You will see more of Subirachs at Gaudí's Sagrada Familia temple.

2 Walk across to the top of the Rambla and the Canaletes fountain.

The Canaletes fountain, about 20 paces down the Rambla on the right, once brought the best water in Barcelona from the Llobregat river that flowed from high in the Pyrenees to the Llobregat delta just south of the city. Small canals or *canaletes* piped the water through the Collserola hills to this public fountain. Canaletes is the scene of tumultuous celebrations of Futbol Club Barcelona league triumphs or any victory over Madrid. When Barcelona's football fortunes wane, clusters of impeccably dressed men across the Rambla angrily debate the whys and wherefores of this national disgrace – a sports version of London's Speakers' Corner. The bronze plaque near the base of the fountain warns that if you drink these waters, you will fall helplessly in love with Barcelona and be eternally condemned to return.

3 Continue another 50 paces down the Rambla to the first street on your left, Carrer de Santa Anna.

The first opening on your left offers two streets. The left fork is Carrer de Santa Anna; the right one is Carrer Canuda. A walk down Carrer de Santa Anna will eventually reveal, on the left, a small cobblestone courtyard with a flower stall at the entrance and a minuscule Romanesque church huddled unhappily against the modern construction behind and nearly all around it. The Santa Anna church is one of Barcelona's four earliest churches along with the Raval's Sant Pau del Camp and Capella de Sant Llàtzer, and the Capella d'en Marcús in the Ribera-Born. A hulking 12th-century early Romanesque miniature, the triple bell tower and the cloister filled with orange trees rank along with the sarcophagus of Spanish fleet captain Miguel de Boera as Santa Anna's finest treasures. De Boera served under Emperor Charles V and stopped the invading French in 1543 in the Roussillon, southern France (aka

9

I

DISTANCE 1.5 miles (2.2km)

ALLOW 2 hours

START Plaça Catalunya Metro

FINISH Liceu Metro

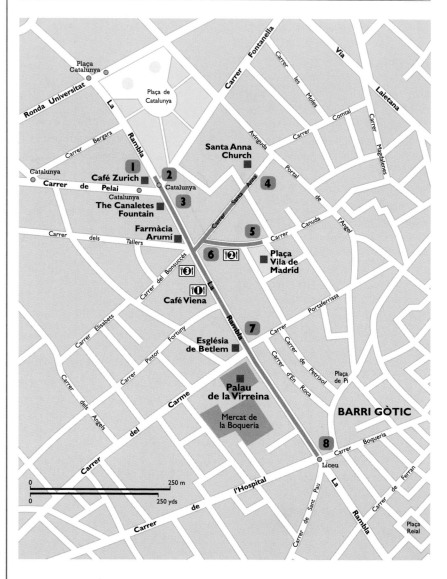

Catalunya Nord). Built in the form of a Greek Cross, the Església de Santa Anna has been linked to the Order of the Knights Templar. Templar crosses – equilateral with arms widening at the ends – are visible on the roof to the right of the apse, over the main entrance, and on the sarcophagus suspended from the southeast wall. Clandestine Templar rituals are said to have taken place here after the order was declared heretical in 1314.

4 Go back to the fork and take Carrer Canuda past the Ateneu barcelonès at No. 6 to the Plaça Vila de Madrid.

Plaça Vila de Madrid is ostensibly a tribute to Barcelona's rival, Spain's upstart capital city. But not so fast: the fact that the square is dedicated to a *vila* or town, rather than to a city, tells us that Madrid's cathedral was unfinished until recently, thus depriving the Spanish capital of authentic city status. Furthermore, the square dedicated to Madrid surrounds a 1st-century Roman road and cemetery, a reminder of Barcelona's 1500-year seniority over the dusty village that only became Spain's royal seat as recently as 1563. The tombs on the lower level of the square include one of a woman interred with her dog. The roadway was the extension of Roman Barcino's main east-west axis. The Ateneu barcelonès, overlooking the square, a private club and library, holds frequent cultural events open to the public; a chance to see the upstairs garden and the antique library, though most polite requests to enter and

WHERE TO EAT

🍴 CAFÉ VIENA,
Rambla dels Estudis 115;
93-349-9800.
The best *flauta* ('flute' of fresh homemade bread) with *jamón ibérico* (Iberian ham) in Barcelona. €

🍴 EL ATENEU,
Carrer Canuda 6;
93-318-5238.
Cuisine from northern Catalonia's volcanic La Garrotxa served in the entryway of Palau Sabasona, the Ateneu barcelonès. €€

🍴 JULIVERT MEU,
Carrer del Bonsuccés 7;
93-318-0343.
Market cuisine with Mediterranean and Catalan favourites. €€

have a look around are granted.
ATENEU BARCELONÈS;
www.ateneubcn.org

5 Walk back out to the Rambla and look at the Farmàcia Arumí across at the corner of Carrer Tallers.

Barcelona's pharmacists seemed to appreciate the hallucinogenic delirium side of Art Nouveau, for which reason Modernism enjoyed particular cachet with pharmacies. The curious Arumí pharmacy at the corner of the Rambla and Carrer Tallers is in the Noucentisme style, which attempted to sober down the ornamental exuberance of Art Nouveau in the early 20th century. Ismael Smith (1886-1972) was the author of this façade, with its curious sculpture of the infant Hercules, mythological founder of Barcelona, and a snake, symbol (with the mixing vial) of pharmacy, suggesting snake oil remedies. Across the street is the famous Boadas cocktail bar, known to have served mojitos and daiquiris to Hemingway himself. A few steps further down the Rambla on the right is the Poliorama theatre, where the young George Orwell (1903-50), as recounted in *Homage to Catalonia*, stood guard in the tower during mutually destructive warfare between Stalinists and Trotskyites during the 1936-39 Spanish Civil War.

6 Continue down the Rambla past the bird vendors to the intersection of Carrer del Carme, La Rambla, and Carrer de Portaferrissa.

Note the clock on the façade of the Teatre Poliorama, traditionally Barcelona's official timepiece, affixed to the Academy of Natural Sciences. The Café Viena is on the right, a simple quadrilateral counter serving famous Iberian ham 'flautas', slender baguettes slathered with tomato squeezings and olive oil. Down Carrer del Bonsuccés is the restaurant Julivert Meu, while just off to the right down Carrer Elisabets, on the corner of Carrer Pintor Fortuny, is the monument to the Catalan painter Marià Fortuny (1838-74). The splendid Hotel 1898 (with a roof garden restaurant open to the public) abuts the Església de Betlem,

a quilted baroque structure with powerful sculptures of biblical scenes on its Carrer del Carme façade. On this section of the Rambla, bird vendors traditionally hawk (as it were) everything from parrots to peacocks, for pet rather than for pot purposes. The opening to the left into Carrer Portaferrissa has a ceramic representation of the Rambla as it looked in the 13th century: a sandy riverbed with a hunter selling ducks, various market stalls, and a view down Carrer Portaferrissa, named, as the text explains, for the 3ft (1m) iron bar attached to it as the standard measure for textiles.

7 Walk further down the Rambla to the Rambla de les Flors.

The Rambla de les Flors has always been one of the Rambla's most popular spots, for its fragrance as well as for the intimacy of the narrowing walkway. It was here that Moderniste Catalan painter Ramón Casas (1866-1932) and several of the Olot school of landscapists met and married winsome flower vendors who later became their models and wives. The Palau de la Virreina at La Rambla 99 contains a cultural information office, an art gallery dedicated to photography, and, on permanent display, the official Barcelona *caps grossos* (big heads) and *gegants* (giants) used for city festivals.

8 From the Rambla de les Flors, the Liceu metro stop is just a few steps ahead, while the nearby Boqueria market beckons. An about-face will return you to the top of the Rambla in five minutes.

OPPOSITE: JOSEP CLARÀ'S DÉESSE: PLAÇA DE CATALUNYA

La Boqueria, Horn of Plenty

The Boqueria market is the soul (and stomach) of the city; the medieval hospital is a Gothic gem, and Hotel Espanya is awash in Art Nouveau.

The Boqueria market is a marketplace, kitchen and rolling cocktail party open to all. After browsing through this celebration of life and produce, a plunge into the medieval Hospital de la Santa Creu reveals one of Barcelona's finest Gothic spaces. Carrer Hospital immerses you in the Raval, Barcelona's multicultural area, redolent of a North African souk. The Sant Agustí church contains the chapel of Santa Rita de Cassia, patron of hopeless causes (especially unhappily married women). Every 22 May lines of women stretch deep into the Raval, waiting to have their roses blessed by Santa Rita. The roses are brushed across the thighs of the crucifixion in the rear of the church, taken home to wither and dry, and crumbled into diminutive hope chests to wait for better times. Hotel Espanya is a Moderniste gem by Palau de la Música Catalana architect Lluís Domènech i Montaner (1850–1923), while the nearby Liceu Opera house store offers musical mementoes on the way to the very heart of the Rambla.

1 Enter the Boqueria from the Rambla de les Flors.

Just inside the market to the right is Bar Pinotxo, the little lunch counter that launched an ocean of culinary ink. Look for the puppet seated nonchalantly on the corner overhead, while the incandescent Juanito Bayén receives his guests as he has for half a century. Everything in the Boqueria is mouthwatering and eye-popping: Quim de la Boqueria is 20 paces in and another 20 to the left, while the sweet red pepper stand just beyond is the most beautiful display in the market. Llorenç Petrás, the wild mushroom czar, is back centre, while the greengrocers' market in Placeta de Sant Galdric is at the upper edge, centre right. Note the Doric columns surrounding the market, from the original mid-19th century neoclassical square designed by Francesc Daniel i Molina (1812–67), sister square to Plaça Reial further down the Rambla.

2 Walk across the parking lot behind the Boqueria to the medieval hospital's Casa de la Convalescencia.

Leave the Boqueria from the Petrás wild mushroom stand, passing the tables of the Gardunya restaurant, time-honoured purveyor of late-night onion soup to opera-goers. Walk right and then left past terrace restaurants into the hospital complex, leaving the monument to Doctor Fleming (1809–79), inventor of penicillin, to your right. The Casa de la Convalescencia (Convalescence House) is in to the right, facing the door of the Royal Academy of Surgery. The vestibule is decorated with original ceramic tiles created in 1680 by tile master Llorenç Passolas, chronicling the life of St Paul. Left of the patio entrance, the first scene, based on the Rubens painting *The Conversion of Saint Paul,* portrays the warrior's conversion. Moving around the vestibule to the left Paul is portrayed preaching, fleeing from Damascus (lowered over the walls in a basket), curing the sick in Lystra, embarking for Ephesus where he wrote his letters (just to the left of the outer door), before the magistrates, imprisoned, writing epistles under an olive tree, and in Rome with St Peter. Finally, we see the saint's decapitation, his head drawing miraculous springs of water on each bounce, as according to legend. The patio inside is one of Barcelona's finest baroque

DISTANCE 1 mile (1.6km)

ALLOW 1.5 hours (more with site visits)

START Upper Liceo Metro station

FINISH Lower Liceo Metro station

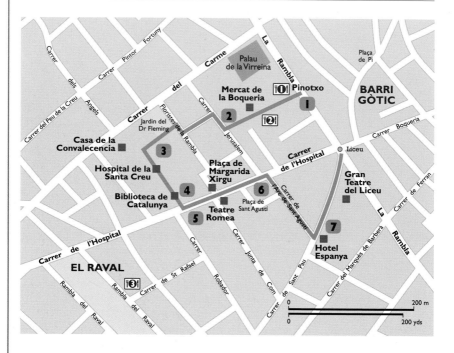

works, built between 1655 and 1678. In the second-floor garden (a popular Mediterranean feature) is a sculpture of St Paul, sword in hand. The horseshoes embedded in the heavy outer door are a reference to the building's benefactor, Pau Ferran, farrier and blacksmith.

3 Turn right and walk through the courtyard of the medieval hospital to the stairway on the right, leading up to the Biblioteca de Catalunya. Notice the sculpture guarding the stairway.

This is Sant Roc, patron saint of the sick, in his pilgrim attire, showing the plague sore on his thigh while his dog carries a loaf of bread (Sant Roc's story stars a dog who supplied him with bread). At the top of the stairs, the Biblioteca de Catalunya is a sweeping Gothic space, one of Barcelona's four finest along with Reial Drassanes, the medieval shipyards; Santa Maria del Mar basilica; and the Saló Gótica in the Llotja de Mar (Maritime Exchange). Founded by Sovereign Count Martí l'Humà (1356–1410) who died

OPPOSITE: GOTHIC ARCHES INSIDE BIBLIOTECA DE CATALUNYA

WHERE TO EAT

|O| PINOTXO,
Boqueria Market
La Rambla 91;
93-317-1731.
The top counter in the Boqueria for
nearly half a century. €€

|O| QUIM DE LA BOQUERIA,
Boqueria Market
La Rambla 91;
93-301-9810.
Pinotxo's only competitor serves
taste-filled market specialities. €€

|O| CASA LEOPOLDO,
Sant Rafael 24;
93-241-3014.
Fine seafood and Catalan cuisine in
the heart of the Raval. €€€

without heir, the Hospital de la Santa
Creu (Hospital of the Holy Cross) was
one of Europe's first multi-disciplinary
hospitals. Antoni Gaudí, struck by a
trolley car on his way to mass at the
Sant Felip Neri church on 7 June 1926,
died at the hospital shortly before it was
moved to the Hospital de Sant Pau on
the far side of the Eixample. The soaring
arches and high windows were designed
to admit abundant light to help cure
the sick, while the modern study carrels
with computer hookups provide access
to more than 500,000 documents in the
library's stacks.
BIBLIOTECA DE CATALUNYA;
TEL: 93/270-2300; www.bcn.es/

4 Continue through the courtyard
and into Carrer Hospital, before
walking left to the corner.

The Escola Massana art school and its
romantic balcony over the corner El Jardí
restaurant lead out into Carrer Hospital.
From the far side of the street, look back
at the hospital façade, with its Holy Cross
crowned with a bat, Catalonia founder
Jaume I's chosen symbol for the House of
Aragón. Gargoyles and griffins peer down
from the top of the façade. Moving left,
back toward the Rambla, is the Capella
del Hospital, the hospital chapel, now
used for art exhibits. The outside bar
on the corner of Carrer de la Junta de
Comerç is popular. Carrer Hospital fills
with natural goods from the countryside
on 11 May, Día de Sant Ponç, patron
saint of beekeepers and herbalists, when
farmers clean out their larders and
healing potions are displayed next to the
hospital walls.

5 Cross Carrer Hospital to Plaça de
Margarida Xirgu. Walk by historic
Teatre Romea into Plaça de Sant Agustí.

The small square to the left across
from the Teatre Romea is dedicated to
Margarida Xirgu, famous stage actress
of the 1920s and 30s and lover, albeit
platonic, of poet and playwright Federico
García Lorca, whose dedication is at the
foot of the Sergi Aguilar sculpture. A little
way past the Teatre Romea is the Plaça de
Sant Agustí, with its half-finished façade,
the upper half rough and rocky, a result of
late 18th-century funding problems.

6 Walk right down Carrer de l'Arc de Sant Agustí to the Hotel Espanya at the end of the street.

The Moderniste Hotel Espanya is one of Barcelona's loveliest and least known Art Nouveau sites. Filled with gorgeous ceramic tiling, murals of mermaids and Mediterranean sea life, and a sculpted fireplace, the Hotel Espanya should be charging admission as a museum when, in fact, it barely charges for rooms as a budget hotel. The dining room is decorated with the heraldry of Spain's regions and provinces, from Sevilla to Navarra. The Eusebi Arnau fireplace in the breakfast room is an allegory of life, from infancy to old age, crowned with Spain's imperial coat of arms.

7 From the Hotel Espanya, walk towards the Rambla. Pass the Gran Teatre del Liceu's back entrance, duck downstairs into the Liceu store and café.

The opera house holds guided tours daily, but a visit to its store and café might be enough to get the idea. The pièce de résistance is the intimate amphitheatre's videos of the Liceu's dramatic thrice-torched history, played along with snatches of opera. A good spot for a rest, the video room leads to the café and up a ramp to the Rambla, just below Pla de la Boqueria, with its Joan Miró mosaic at the centre of the intersection and the lower entrance to the Liceu metro.
GRAN TEATRE DEL LICEU;
TEL: 93/485-9998; www.liceubarcelona.com

ABOVE: GRAN TEATRE DEL LICEU

The Mediterranean end of the Rambla

The lower Rambla, from the Liceu opera house to the port, has it all: neoclassical order, Modernisme, streetwalkers and Gothic splendour.

As it descends, the Rambla changes character. From the banks, department stores, and cultural centres at the upper end; through the flowers, food, and musical treasures in the middle, the final stretch leading down to the port offers seamier nightlife, elegant formal squares, Gaudí architecture, art galleries and the Gothic shipyard where the Catalan fleet was built between the 13th and 16th centuries. Off to its left and right are Plaça Reial, a mid-19th century neoclassical square struggling to live up to its orderly rational design; Gaudí's Palau Güell, one of the great Moderniste's most singular creations; Carrer Escudellers with its bars, clubs and ceramics shops; and the Santa Monica art gallery built in a former convent. Street life on the lower Rambla is even more colourful than that of the upper. The most creative street performers tend to set up just beyond the opera house, as do portrait painters and tarot readers, while, off to either side, human commerce has been raging for centuries.

1 Start at the colourful Joan Miró mosaic in Pla de la Boqueria.

The pavement cafés just below the Liceu opera house attract new visitors, but savvy *barcelonins* steer a wide berth around the inflated prices and poor food, though watching the waiters dodging taxis and motorbikes as they bus trays out to the terrace is good sport. The Café de l'Opera across from the Liceu is a traditional Rambla meeting point. Thonet chairs, acid-engraved antique mirrors, the semi-clandestine back door, and the lived-in feel of the place all contribute to the café's charm. The Hotel Internacional overlooking Pla de la Boqueria is a Rambla landmark, its 1894 founding date proudly atop the façade. A hundred years later, while the Liceu was being gutted by fire, Catalan soprano Montserrat Caballé watched in tears from the hotel balcony while her beloved opera house burned. A short stroll down the Rambla on the right is Hotel Oriente, its angels – reminders of the 16th-century Sant Àngel Màrtir convent – playing fanfare over the door of what was once Barcelona's finest hotel. The Oriente lodged, among other luminaries, Hans Christian Andersen, King Alfonso XIII (grandfather of Spain's King Juan Carlos I), Errol Flynn, Maria Callas, Ava Gardner, Ernest Hemingway and Spanish bullfight martyr Manolete. The street performers here, in the reflected glory of the opera, seem more creative and inspired than those on the stodgier upper end of the Rambla; joining any throng a busker has managed to attract is often a good idea.

2 Turn left into Plaça Reial beyond Hotel Oriente.

Plaça Reial is a neoclassical square with a Bohemian attitude palpable in its tropical palm trees and motley array of residents. It was named for Queen Isabel II, who reigned from 1833 to 1868, the child queen named by King Fernando VII in defiance of the Salic laws prohibiting women from royal succession. The subsequent Carlist wars in favour of the monarchical rights of Don Carlos, brother of Fernando VII, defined the original standoff between 'the two Spains' – one liberal, secular and progressive, the other authoritarian, religious and reactionary – that killed nearly a million during the 1936-39 Spanish Civil War and which, as the 2008 elections demonstrated, remains unreconciled.

21

OPPOSITE: THREE GRACES FOUNTAIN IN PLAÇA REIAL; ABOVE: ENTRANCE TO THE HOTEL ORIENTE

DISTANCE **1 mile (1.6km)**

ALLOW **2.5 hours**

START **Liceu Metro**

FINISH **Drassanes Metro**

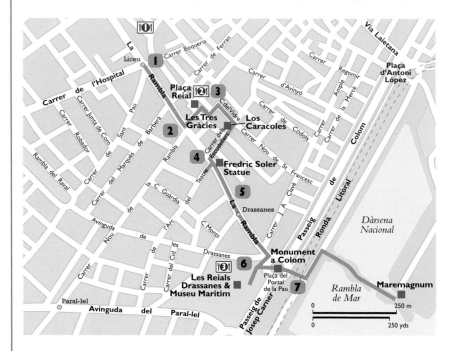

Plaça Reial's central fountain, Les Tres Gràcies – The Three Graces, Aglaia (Beauty), Euphrosyne (Happiness) and Thalia (Charm) – stands between lamp posts designed by a 26-year-old Antoni Gaudí in 1878. The spiky lamp and the winged helmet show little of Gaudí, though the gaping-mouthed serpents confirm that the eccentric master was lurking within. Looking back out to the Rambla, two pairs of cherubs are silhouetted against the sky at either side, supporting royal crowns and the coats of arms of León and Castile, the realms which, when combined with Aragón and Catalonia, formed the modern Spanish state after the marriage of Ferdinand of Aragón and Isabella of Castile in 1469. Underneath are medallions commemorating Spain's great mariners, explorers and conquistadors: Cortés, Pizarro, Magellan, Elkano and Cisneros.

3 Walk out the far right corner of Plaça Reial through Carrer Vidre to the corner of Carrer Escudellers, turn right again and walk back out to the Rambla.

At the intersection of Carrer Vidre (named for glass blowers) and Carrer dels Escudellers (potters), roasting chickens on spits mark Los Caracoles, for years Barcelona's most famous restaurant. A loop through the bar and open kitchen and out the side door to the right is usually permitted by the generous Bofarull family. The fresh fish, snails (*caracoles*) and roast suckling pig or lamb here are excellent. Back in Carrer dels Escudellers, the Art Escudellers ceramics stores at the corner and across the street at No. 23-25 show and sell excellent wares from all over Spain. The Art Nouveau Grill Room at No. 8 has a gorgeous wooden bar, a good place for a libation. Back on the Rambla is the seated statue of 19th-century playwright Frederic Soler (1839-95), known as Pitarra, the father of modern Catalan theatre, across from the Teatre Principal where Barcelona's earliest theatre stood in 1568.

4 Walk across the Rambla for a closer look at the Teatre Principal façade, ducking into Carrer de l'Arc del Teatre and then down to the Centre d'Art de Santa Mònica.

This part of the Rambla has traditionally been prime habitat for the overflow from the Barrio Chino's most louche corners, as a look up Carrer de l'Arc del Teatre, past the tiny clandestine street bar Quiosco de la Cazalla tucked just inside

WHERE TO EAT

🍴 TABERNA BASCA IRATI,
Cardenal Casañas 17;
93-302-3084.
Tapas up front and excellent Basque fare in the back. €€

🍴 TAXIDERMISTA,
Plaça Reial 8;
93-412-4536.
The only respectable restaurant in Plaça Reial. €€

🍴 RESTAURANTE DE LES DRASSANES,
Av. de les Drassanes s/n;
93-318-0215.
Postmodern Mediterranean cuisine under Gothic arches. €€

off the Rambla, will confirm. The Centre d'Art de Santa Mònica, a modern art gallery and bookstore, is just down the Rambla attached to the 1618 convent of the Agustins Descalços de Santa Mònica.

5 Continue down the Rambla to the Reials Drassanes shipyards.

On Plaça del Portal de la Pau, Les Reials Drassanes, the medieval shipyards and Maritime Museum, is superb late 14th-century Catalan Gothic architecture and the best-preserved medieval shipyards in the world. Drassanes built Catalonia's Mediterranean fleet and launched the ships directly down their slipways into the sea (today's port leaving Drassanes

23

landlocked is landfill). Around the outside on the Avinguda del Paral.lel you will see a perfectly intact section of the 14th- to 15th-century city walls.

6 Cross to the Rambla from Drassanes and then to the Columbus Monument in the Plaça del Portal de la Pau.

The Columbus Monument towers over the foot of the Rambla as if he were the city's founder or favourite son. Columbus,

however, has his back to the city: a bad sign. Catalonia and 'The Discoverer' have never seen eye to eye. Ferdinand and Isabella sponsored Columbus's voyage; the Drassanes shipyards constructed two of Columbus's ships; Columbus 'discovered' America and brought the good news and a few unhappy Arawaks back to the itinerant royal court in Barcelona, whereupon the Spanish crown excluded Catalonia from New World trade, confining her to the Mediterranean. Catalans hold long grudges, especially

ABOVE: DRASSANES AND MUSEU MARITIM

over commercial slights. Standing atop his iron pedestal, Columbus appears to be looking towards the new world he found, though in fact his finger is pointing southeast at the Mediterranean, Barcelona's once and future trading grounds. For panoramic views, take the elevator to the top of the column.

7 From the Columbus Monument cross to the port side of Plaça Portal de la Pau to the ornate customs building and the wooden Rambla de Mar.

On Moll Drassanes stands the wedding cake-like Duana, or customs building, built in 1895. Next door are the ticket windows for Las Golondrinas, the passenger boats that tour the harbour and sail up the coast to the Olympic Port and the Fòrum complex. The Rambla de Mar, the wooden boardwalk and drawbridge over to the Maremagnum shopping complex, leads out to the Aquarium and the IMAX theatre.

The Drassanes metro stop is just a short stroll back up the Rambla.

THE COLUMBUS MONUMENT, PLAÇA DEL PORTAL DE LA PAU

Roman Barcelona: the Yolk of the Egg

A close look at a Barcelona street map shows, at its centre, an egg-shaped tracery of streets around the high ground occupied by the Cathedral.

The Roman settlement established after 133 BC occupied the high ground overlooking the port that became known as Mons Taber, a knobby mound rising above the surrounding alleys and squares and the sea. This route around the Roman walls, parts of which are still visible, also explores the cathedral and parts of the Gothic Quarter that sprang up inside the Roman walls over the succeeding centuries as Visigoths and Franks filled the void left by the Romans. The Catedral de la Seu is the focus of this walk, with its ecclesiastical outbuildings often more aesthetically memorable than the cathedral itself. The one-time Roman Forum is now Plaça Sant Jaume, where the government seats of Barcelona and Catalonia face each other across the square, while the colossal Corinthian columns of the Temple of Augustus close this exploration of the Roman Colonia Favencia Julia Augusta Paterna Barcino.

1 Start in Plaça Nova to the right of the cathedral façade, a 10-minute walk from the Plaça de Catalunya metro.

Barcelona's cathedral was built between the 13th and 19th centuries, with parts of it (the spiky Gothic façade) not completed until the 20th. To the right of the main façade, at the right edge of the Casa de l'Ardiaca (the Archdeacon's House) are remains of the original aqueduct. Across the front of the cathedral are four of the 82 rectangular Roman watchtowers built in the 4th century when Visigothic pressure from the north ended the Pax Romana.

2 Walk up Carrer del Bisbe to the first corner and turn left into the Casa de l'Ardiaca.

Up the ramp is the entrance to the Roman city between two of the three cylindrical watchtowers built to guard corners. The Arxiu Històric de la Ciutat (City Historical Archive) is installed in what was originally the Archdeacon's house. Through the handsome patio in the reception area are the 4th-century walls with the aqueduct section to the left. Note the carved stones recycled from other buildings thrown hastily into the ramparts in pre-invasion panic.

3 Walk across to the front door of the cathedral and take a stroll through the penumbra within.

Known as the darkest of all of the world's great cathedrals, the space seems larger

WHERE TO EAT

🍴 COMETACINC,
Carrer Cometa 5;
93-310-1558.
Modern Catalan cuisine served in a graceful setting. €€

🍴 CAFÉ DE l'ACADÈMIA,
Carrer Lledó 1;
93-319-8253.
Light Mediterranean fare at the corner of Plaça Sant Just. €€

🍴 COL.LEGI d'ARQUITECTES DE CATALUNYA,
Plaça Nova 5;
93-306-7850.
Surprisingly good Catalan home cooking in the architects' guild. €€€

than it is. Highlights are the Santa Eulàlia high relief sculptures chronicling the young Christian's torture and execution at the hands of Roman consul Decius in the year 303. Santa Eulàlia's tomb is in the cathedral crypt. Behind the Santa Eulàlia reliefs are the wooden choir stalls with 60 wood sculptures of the heads of men and women along the outside. To the left, over the door out into Carrer Comtes, is the intricately sculpted organ loft, while across the nave is the entrance to the leafy cloister with its flock of 13 geese said to represent, in their whiteness, Santa Eulàlia's purity, and, in their number, the 13 ordeals that Decius inflicted upon her. The Santa Llúcia chapel is around to the right, leading you

DISTANCE **1.5 miles (3.2km)**

ALLOW **2.5 hours**

START **Plaça Nova**

FINISH **Plaça Sant Jaume**

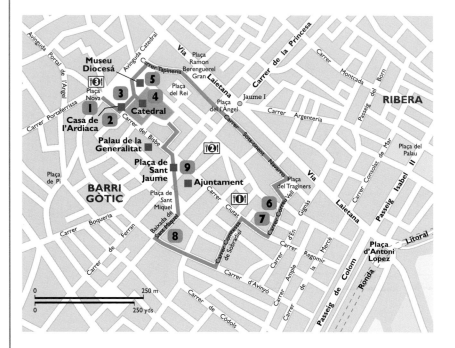

back out to the Casa de l'Ardiaca once more.

4 Retrace your steps across the front of the cathedral and go down the steps to the Casa de la Pia Almoina, the Museu Diocesà, on the right.

The octagonal watchtower that contains the Diocesan Museum is the only one of its kind. The design of the stairways and platforms inside the Roman stone structure is as interesting as the temporary

and permanent displays here. On the top floor a film on Gaudí is narrated, in English, with the architect's thoughts on his own work.

5 Move left around the walls along Carrer Tapineria past Plaça Ramon Berenguer el Gran and through Plaça de l'Àngel into Carrer del Sots-Tinent Navarro to Plaça dels Traginers.

Roman watchtowers, restored so the original Montjuïc sandstone is easily

distinguishable from the bricks used to reinforce and fill gaps, take you around to the equestrian statue dedicated to Ramon Berenguer el Gran, under whose 1097-1131 rule independent Catalonia reached its pinnacle of historical greatness, with its fleet spread across the Mediterranean as far as Greece, and new lands acquired from the Pyrenees to Provence. Continuing through Plaça de l'Àngel and into Carrer del Sots-Tinent Navarro, Roman watchtowers lead around to Plaça dels Traginers, named for medieval cart makers. Another cylindrical watchtower overlooks the Mediterranean corner of the Roman enclosure on what was the edge of the beach before landfill forced the coastline back.

6 Walk ahead through Carrer Correu Vell past the back entrance to the Pati Llimona civic centre and around to Carrer Regomir. Halfway down Carrer Correu Vell an opening to the right reveals a large expanse of Roman wall. At the next corner, turn right on Carrer Regomir and walk up to the tiny and picturesque Sant Cristófol chapel.

Next to the chapel, a window and glass panel in the pavement show the Roman Portal del Mar, the waterfront entrance to Barcino. Inside, the large carriage port can be seen fallen over, with the two smaller entryways to either side.

7 Cross Carrer Regomir and walk through Carrer Comtessa de Sobradiel to the corner of Carrer d'Avinyó and go right.

Carrer d'Avinyó, where a late 19th-century brothel inspired Picasso's seminal painting *Les Demoiselles d'Avignon*, passes La Llotja design school at the corner of Carrer de Cervantes. Across the street are excellent *sgraffito* designs. This decorative technique, in which a top layer of colour is scratched off to reveal the colour beneath, was widely used in 18th-century Barcelona. At No. 19 is a small restaurant with a back room where you can have lunch between two perfectly preserved Roman watchtowers. Upstairs, next door, is the Asociació Excursionista, Expedicionari, i Folklòric (AEEF) where, from 7-9pm every weekday evening but Thursday, visitors can stroll between the 1st and 4th-century Roman walls discovered beneath the plaster walls of the main meeting room. This unique look at the two walls reveals the lighter 1st-century ritual wall used primarily to mark the city limits, and the heavy defensive 4th-century wall containing recycled fragments of carved building stones thrown in as quickly as possible.

8 Turn right at the next corner up Baixada de Sant Miquel, through Plaça de Sant Miquel, and into Plaça Sant Jaume, once the Roman Forum.

Walking up Baixada de Sant Miquel past Palau Centelles, have a look into this gorgeous Renaissance courtyard. Plaça Sant Jaume spreads out between the Barcelona Town Hall and the Generalitat de Catalunya, the seat of government of Catalonia. The Town Hall, filled with sculptures and murals, can be visited on Saturday and Sunday mornings. The Generalitat is open to the public only on rare holidays or by special arrangement. The Roman Forum once occupied this space, though about three times more of it, at the intersection of the two north–south and east–west Roman arteries, Decumanus Maximus and Cardo Maximo.

9 Cross Plaça Sant Jaume, leaving Carrer del Bisbe to your left, turn right up Carrer Paradís and walk around the first corner to the Centre Excursionista de Catalunya (CEC).

The perfectly preserved fluted 2nd-century columns from the Roman Temple of Augustus, visible in the entryway of the Centre Excursionista de Catalunya, were concealed by modern construction until the early 20th century. The Temple of Augustus occupied part of the Roman Forum, as the exhibit inside makes clear. For more of Roman Barcelona, a walk through the Museu d'Història de la Ciutat in nearby Plaça del Rei is recommended. The nearest metro stop is Jaume I on Via Laietana, but the most practical transport hub is at Plaça Catalunya, 10 minutes away.

ABOVE: THE AJUNTAMENT (TOWN HALL) ACROSS PLAÇA DE SANT JAUME

The Gothic Quarter

The Gothic Quarter closes out the urban roar, allowing classical guitar, flute and cello to resonate through stone spaces and intimate squares.

Barcelona's Gothic Quarter winds through a maze of narrow streets and tiny squares between the Rambla on the southwest side and Via Laietana on the northeast edge. Antiques stores, art galleries, fashion stores, delicatessens, museums, cafés, tapas bars and restaurants all vie for time and attention here: a thorough exploration of the Barri Gòtic could take a week. In two or three hours you can see some of what there is to see, though the visits to the City History or Frederic Marès museums will double or even triple your time. Curiously, none of Barcelona's four finest Gothic structures – Santa Maria del Mar basilica, Reials Drassanes shipyards, La Llotja maritime exchange, and the Medieval Hospital – are in the Gothic Quarter, and some of what is in the quarter is either Renaissance or neo-Gothic. The tiny alleys of the Jewish Quarter, the shops along Carrer Banys Nous, and the soothing hush of these pedestrian byways all deliver the intimate caress of time standing still: if the Rambla is flux, the Gothic Quarter is stasis.

Start at the corner of Carrer
Portaferrissa and Petritxol just
off the Rambla.

Carrer Petritxol is one of Barcelona's
most popular streets, a succession of
art galleries and hot chocolate shops
irresistible on rainy winter afternoons.
At No. 5, Sala Parés is the dean of
Barcelona's art galleries, a wood-floored
space with lingering aromas of oil paints
and time. Ramón Casas, Isidre Nonell,
Pablo Picasso, and Santiago Rusinyol all
showed here. At No. 2 is the Llibreria
Querol, specialists in hiking literature
and maps of the Pyrenees. At the end of
the street, the giant rose window of the
Església de Santa Maria del Pi looms over
Plaça del Pi, named for an ancestor of the
present pine. The decaying building to
the right is the Casa de la Sang (House
of Blood) named for the Cofradia de
la Sang (Brotherhood of the Blood of
Christ) charged with preparing prisoners
condemned to death. The Ganivetería
Roca on the corner is Barcelona's top
cutlery store, with the city's earliest and
best-preserved *sgraffito* (see page 32)
designs on the façade.

2 Browse through Plaça del Pi and the
adjoining Plaça de Sant Josep Oriol
before walking down Carrer de la Palla
to the corner of Carrer Banys Nous.

Plaça del Pi holds a farmers' market every
Thursday with organic produce from
the countryside, while neighbouring
Plaça Sant Josep Oriol has a weekend art
market. The bronze effigy is of 19th-

WHERE TO EAT

🍴 TALLER DE TAPAS,
Plaça Sant Josep Oriol 9;
93-301-8020.
A wide variety of tapas and wines
next to the Església del Pi. €€

🍴 L'HOSTAL DEL PINTOR,
Carrer Sant Honorat 6;
93-301-4065.
Graceful décor and light Catalan
cooking in the shadow of the Palau
de la Generalitat. €€

century playwright Àngel Guimerà.
Taller de Tapas is in to the right, while
Carrer de la Palla leads left past several
art galleries and antique stores to the
corner of Carrer Banys Nous, so-named
for the Jewish baths that once occupied
the basement of the Caelum café on
the corner. A detour to the left will take
you to the Artur Ramón art galleries
and antique shops. Down Carrer Banys
Nous to the right is L'Arca de L'Àvia
(Grandmother's Trunk), specializing in
vintage fashions. The tiles overhead to the
right depict frolicking men and women
in the Jewish baths, although, in fact,
Jewish baths were never mixed sex.

3 Walk up the Baixada de Santa
Eulàlia to the first left turn into
Plaça de Sant Felip Neri.

Named for the hill where, in 303 AD,
Roman Consul Decius rolled Santa
Eulàlia in a barrel filled with shards of

37

DISTANCE **1.2 miles (3.2km)**

ALLOW **2.5 hours**

START **Corner of Carrers Portaferrissa and Petritxol**

FINISH **Plaça Sant Just**

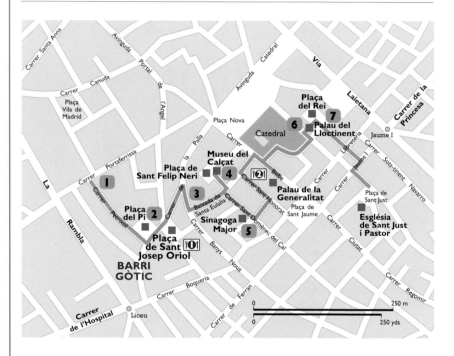

glass (one of the 13 ordeals designed to persuade her to recant her Christian faith), Baixada de Santa Eulàlia has a small chapel to Eulàlia overhead to the right. A few steps on is Carrer Sant Felip Neri, leading left into a small square. Hotel Neri is on the corner. The shrapnel marks on the wall of the baroque church were left by a Franco bomb dropped into the square in 1938, killing a number of schoolchildren. The Museu del Calçat, the cobbler's guild and museum, stands on the right side of the square.

4 Retrace your steps to Carrer Sant Domènec del Call, the entrance to the medieval Jewish Quarter.

The historical plaque on Carrer Sant Sever explains the history of the Barcelona Call or Jewish Quarter, destroyed in 1391 a full century before the official Expulsion Decree with which the Catholic monarchs Ferdinand and Isabella resolved Spain's religious conflicts after defeating the last Moorish dynasty at Granada. Walk into Carrer Sant

OPPOSITE: CARRER DE FERRAN: BARRI GÒTIC

Domènec del Call to Placeta Manuel Ribé. Through Carrer Sant Domenec del Call on the corner of Carrer Marlet is the Sinagoga Major, the main synagogue of Barcelona's medieval Jewish community. **EL CALL;** www.calldebarcelona.org

5 From the synagogue, walk across Sant Domènec del Call through Carrer Fruita to Carrer Sant Honorat. A left turn leads past the Hostal del Pintor restaurant, back to Carrer Sant Sever.

The tiny Església de Sant Sever just across Carrer Sant Sever has the city's finest gilded baroque altar. Continuing to Carrer del Bisbe, and turning right, you will see the much-mocked neo-Gothic 'Bridge of Sighs' overpass connecting the Palau de la Generalitat with its office buildings. This façade of the Palau de la Generalitat, originally the main Gothic façade, is worth a short detour to peruse, with its representation of St George slaying the dragon over the door. Back at the corner of the cathedral, the walk through Carrer Pietat leads around the apse of the cathedral, under a menagerie of zoological gargoyles to the Palau del Lloctinet (Lieutenant's Palace), the archive of the Corona de Aragón. A few steps further on is the Museu Frederic Marès, a collection of art and miscellanea covering everything from 12th-century wood carvings to 20th-century walking sticks. The café in the leafy courtyard between Roman watchtowers is a good refreshment stop.

MUSEU FREDERIC MARÈS;

www.museumares.bcn.es

6 Walk back through the Palau del Lloctinent into the beautiful and historic Plaça del Rei.

The Palau del Lloctinent patio has ceilings and a bronze door by Josep Maria Subirachs, the sculptor charged with finishing Gaudí's Sagrada Familia church. The museum chronicles the life and writings of James I The Conqueror, father of the Catalonian nation. Plaça del Rei, where classical guitarists lend a musical dimension to stunning architecture, is surrounded by the watchtower of King Martí I on the left, the Saló del Tinell inside, and the Capella Reial de Santa Àgata to the right, all part of the Royal Palace used before the itinerant royal court was established in Madrid in 1561. The bronze sculpture is *Topo* ('Space' in Greek) by Basque sculptor Eduardo Chillida (1924-2002).

7 Walk out of Carrer del Veguer, cross Carrer Llibreteria and Carrer Jaume I, and hook right before turning left up Carrer Dagueria into Plaça de Sant Just.

Carrer del Veguer passes the Museu d'Història de la Ciutat, a stroll through Roman Barcelona. Carrer Dagueria leads to Scotswoman Katherine McLaughlin's superb La Seu cheese shop at No. 16, the best place for cheese, wine and olive oil. The Església de Sant Just i Pastor was at one point home of the beloved Black Virgin of Montserrat.

The Jaume I metro stop on Via Laietana is the closest, but Plaça Catalunya, 10 minutes away, is more useful.

Barri de Sant Pere: the Early Textile District

This area was once the textile district, where looms turned Iberia's wool monopoly into fabrics sold throughout Europe and the Mediterranean.

This walk past (or better, through) the Moderniste flagship, El Palau de la Música Catalana, begins in Plaça Catalunya and winds through the upper edge of the Gothic Quarter before plunging into the quiet streets of the Barri de Sant Pere, the medieval textile district. Els 4Gats, the café where late-19th and early 20th-century artists and architects from Picasso to Gaudí gathered in the Cercle Artístic de Sant Lluc, is just an aperitif for the stupendous Palau de la Música Catalana, a music venue where excitement reaches fever pitch before the first note even sounds. The streets around the Barri de Sant Pere offer a look into the heart of a historic area where tourists are the exception rather than the rule and life goes on much the way it has for centuries. The Mercat de Santa Caterina, a state-of-the-art produce market with an innovative and eclectic restaurant, is another look at Barcelona's will to embrace new design and technology without sacrificing history or aesthetics.

Start in Plaça de Catalunya and walk to Avinguda Porta del Àngel at the northeast corner of the square.

Plaça Catalunya has been Barcelona's transport hub since 1927. Metro and bus lines leave from beneath and around this ample and, for the most part, charmless space dominated by the cruise ship-like El Corte Inglés, Spain's ultimate department store, on the north side and the Triangle D'Or (Golden Triangle) shopping mall on the opposite side, behind the Café Zurich. Plaça Catalunya has witnessed three of the 20th century's seminal moments: Franco's occupation of Barcelona in 1939, when his rebel army marched in and removed the Plaça de Catalunya signs in favour of Plaza del Ejército

(Army Square); the 11 September 1977 marking of La Diada, the first celebration of Catalonia's national day since 1939; and the 17 October 1987 announcement that Barcelona had been chosen to host the 1992 Olympic Games, when the city collapsed in joy, schools closed, traffic stopped, complete strangers embraced, the telephone system went down, and Plaça Catalunya filled with office workers (including those from Telefónica) in a dancing, howling celebration. Barcelona's Olympic dream had come true, Catalonia had finally arrived, Madrid was, for once, trumped. The city's modern future began that day.

2 Walk down Avinguda Porta del Àngel to the corner of Carrer Montsió and turn left to Els 4Gats café.

DISTANCE **1.5 miles (4km)**

ALLOW **3 hours**

START **Plaça Catalunya**

FINISH **Mercat de Santa Caterina**

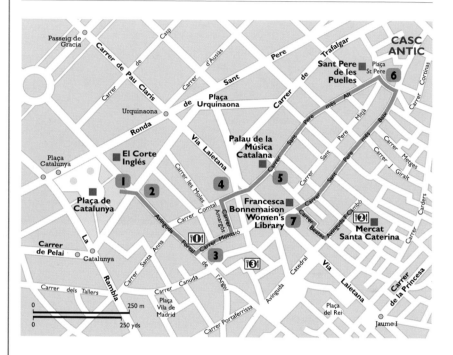

After passing the Pau Gargallo bronze *Shepherd Playing a Flute* on the northeast corner of Plaça Catalunya, the wide Porta del Àngel shopping street, usually filled with avid shoe shoppers from all over Spain, leads down to Carrer Montsió, home of Els 4Gats, Barcelona's most famous café. At No. 3 bis, Casa Martí, an intensely sculpted facade designed in 1895 by Josep Puig i Cadafalch, Modernism's most prolific architect, is a perfect setting for an artistic hangout frequented by the likes of Pablo Picasso,

Isidre Nonell, Antoni Gaudí, Ramón Casas, Rubén Darío, Isaac Albéniz, and Santiago Rusinyol: anything but 'practically no one', which is what *quatre gats* (four cats) means in Catalan. Picasso hung his first show here on 1 February 1900 to mixed reviews praising his draughtsmanship while panning 'Picazzo' as lacking in originality. The Ramón Casas mural of lanky 4Gats founder Pere Romeu on a double bicycle with the Toulouse Lautrec-like (in physique and artistic style) Casas dominates the front

room. Eusebi Arnau sculptures outside include St George killing the dragon and a new-looking Joseph with infant Jesus – a replacement for the sculpture pulled down by anti-clerical anarchists at the start of the Spanish Civil War (1936-39).

3 Walk down Carrer Montsió to the corner of Carrer Amargós and turn left. Walk through Carrer Amargós to the corner of Carrer Comtal and turn right out to Via Laietana.

Carrer Montsió leads past one of the world's last traditional barbershops for men (at No. 9) and the back of the Balmesiana Library on the right before Carrer Amargós enters from the left. This narrow lane is lined with rustic taverns and shops, beginning with the diminutive Mercè Vins at No.1-3. A right turn on Carrer Comtal leads out to Via Laietana where, on the corner of Carrer de Sant Pere Més Alt (Upper Saint Peter's Street) across to the right is the spectacular Gremi de Velers, the Silkweavers' Guild, with superb *sgraffito* (see page 32) designs. Silkweavers were respected on a par with silversmiths and engravers in textile-avid medieval Barcelona; the guild was founded in 1553.

4 Cross Via Laietana at the crossing to the right and walk into Carrer Sant Pere Més Alt.

The explosion of colour and form ahead is the Palau de la Música Catalana, designed by Lluís Domènech i Montaner in 1905. Conceived by the founding

Orfeó Catalá as a home for popular music, as opposed to the elitist and aristocratic opera tradition of the Liceu, the Miquel Blay sculpture over the far corner represents the Palau's commitment to Catalan folklore and culture. St George the dragon slayer, young maidens and seamen with oars spreading Catalan folklore across the seas all cluster together. The busts overhead are of Palestrina, Bach, Beethoven, and, on the east side, Wagner. At the top of the façade is the Orfeó Catalá Choral Society. The interior is even more tumultuous, with Wagnerian cavalry bursting out of the woodwork and an inverted polychrome chandelier skylight descending from on high bringing the cosmic gift of music to earth and the paying public. Guided tours in English can be booked at the ticket office around to the left.

PALAU DE LA MÚSICA CATALANA; www.palaumusica.org

5 Continue down Carrer Sant Pere Més Alt to the church of Sant Pere de les Puelles.

The first house on the right at No. 18 is known as the House of the Four Seasons. The façade is decorated with graceful *sgraffito* designs depicting cherubs weaving garlands, harvesting wheat, cutting grapes, and roasting chestnuts. Palau Dou at No. 27, a neoclassical 19th-century stone façade, was the home of one of Barcelona's important textile families. One-time mansions and palaces built by textile barons, now divided into apartments, line Carrer Sant Pere Més Alt all the way down to the Sant Pere de les Puelles church at the end of the street.

6 Continue through Plaça de Sant Pere to Carrer de Sant Pere Més Baix (Lower Saint Peter's Street) and walk to the Francesca Bonnemaison women's library at No. 7.

Carrer Sant Pere Més Baix is notable for little other than its working class and increasingly multicultural identity. The Palau dels Marquesos d'Alòs at No. 55 is an impressive 17th-century townhouse built by the Dou family. The Farmacia Pedrell at No. 52 is the oldest in Barcelona, founded in 1562. At No. 46 is the 15th-century Casa de les Cortinatges (House of the Curtains) with *sgraffito* designs of cherubs drawing drapes. Near the end of the street at No. 7 is the Biblioteca Popular de la Dona (Woman's Library), founded in 1909 to promote feminine literacy. A Ramon Llull quote: 'Tota dona val mes quan letra apren' (Every woman is worth more when she learns to read) dominates the reading room.

7 Walk across the street through Carrer de les Beates and Plaça de les Beates to Av. Francesc Cambó.

Look to your left for a view of the undulating polychrome roof of the Santa Caterina market. The late Enric Miralles (1955-2000), designer of the Scottish Parliament building, planned a revolutionary marketplace that was finished after his death by his widow,

WHERE TO EAT

🍴 **4GATS,**
Carrer Montsió 3 bis;
93-302-4140.
Spectacular and historic décor and surroundings for simple fare. €€

🍴 **CUINES MERCAT DE SANTA CATERINA,**
Av. Francesc Cambó 20;
93-268-9918.
Eclectic cuisines from around the world with fresh market produce. €€

🍴 **NONELL,**
Plaça Isidre Nonell s/n;
93-301-1378.
Mediterranean and Catalan cooking in a contemporary setting. €€

architect Benedetta Tagliabue. From the mosaic roof with colours evoking Gaudí and Miró motifs to the glass floor panels revealing the original convent beneath, this is a refreshingly different Barcelona market space and a successful fusion of old and new. The restaurant area consists of counters and dining areas offering a range of cuisines from Catalan to Mediterranean to Asian. Meat and vegetable stands remain the market's prime attraction, though a supermarket with home delivery and an online ordering system have created an ultra-modern market housed between neoclassical walls and Visigothic ruins. From the market, the Plaça Catalunya metro is a 10-minute walk.

PALAU DE LA MÚSICA CATALANA, AN EXPLOSION OF COLOUR AND FORM

Catalonia's Cathedral

Santa Maria and the Born-Ribera neighbourhood offer the city's most medieval corners as well as a funky assortment of shops and bars.

From the intersection of Via Laietana and Carrer Argenteria the delicate towers of Santa Maria del Mar are visible at the far end of Carrer Argenteria. Barcelona's most beloved and emblematic church, an early Mediterranean Gothic masterpiece of symmetry and light, is the centrepiece for an area that contains much of medieval Barcelona's most characteristic ancient buildings and alleyways. Once at the very edge of the sea before landfill pushed the shoreline out to Barceloneta and beyond, the Barri de la Ribera, or waterfront district, was outside the Roman walls, a bustling community of stevedores, fishermen, seafarers and tradesmen of every kind. The streets, named for makers of swords, hoods, hats, blankets, pots, glass and all manner of goods, are now densely populated with shops, bars, restaurants and the ancient and eccentric quirks and corners of the medieval heart of this steamy Mediterranean seaport.

I Start at the Jaume I metro stop, the intersection of Via Laietana and Carrer Argenteria, and walk down toward Santa Maria del Mar.

Carrer Argenteria, named for the medieval silversmiths who once worked along this busy artery leading down into the Born-Ribera neighbourhood, is lined with shops, bars and a boutique hotel, Hotel Banys Orientals. Senyor Parellada is a worthy place for dinner if you can get a table in the elegant central patio. Probes to the left of Carrer Argenteria reveal craft shops in beautifully restored spaces, such as Capricho de Muñeca at Carrer Brosolí 1 or La Barcelana next door under the same number. Taller de Tapas and Sagardí are two tapas specialists across the street from each other. Santa Maria del Mar is at the end of the street in Plaça de Santa Maria.

2 Walk into Santa Maria del Mar basilica (closed 1:30-4:30pm) and explore the interior.

The paradigm of early Mediterranean Gothic architecture, Santa Maria del Mar (St Mary of the Sea), is where every *barcelonin* and *barcelonina* wants to be married. The clean lines and balance, the upsweeping elegance, and the abundant and ever-changing Mediterranean light streaming through the stained glass high on the eastern façade are spellbinding. The basilica was built to protect the Catalan fleet following Jaume I's pledge, after conquering Majorca from the Moors in 1229, of a church in exchange

WHERE TO EAT

🍽️ CAL PEP,
Plaça de les Olles 8;
93-310-7961.
The best deep-fried seafood and tapas counter in Barcelona. €€

🍽️ EL PASSADIS D'EN PEP,
Pla del Palau 2-3;
93-310-1021.
Cousin to Cal Pep: more elegant seafood specialists. €€€

🍽️ ORIGENS 99.9%,
Carrer Vidrieria 6-8;
93-310-7531.
Carefully researched medieval Catalan recipes using local ingredients. €€

for divine intervention in battle. His great-grandson Alfons III laid the first stone in 1329. Built in just 54 years (1329-83), the roof is supported by slender octagonal pillars opening into rib vaulting. Ironically, much of the basilica's present elegance is the result of the anti-clerical fury of anarchists, who torched it on 18 July 1936 at the start of the Spanish Civil War. Side chapels, choir stalls and royal boxes burned for 11 days until only the original structure was standing. The post-Bauhaus architects who restored the church, influenced by minimalists Walter Gropius and Mies van der Rohe, recognized the purity of stonemason Berenguer de Montagut's original design. Details to

OPPOSITE: DETAIL OF THE VAULTS INSIDE SANTA MARIA DEL MAR

DISTANCE 1 mile (1.6km)

ALLOW 2.5 hours

START Metro Jaume I

FINISH Plaça del Palau

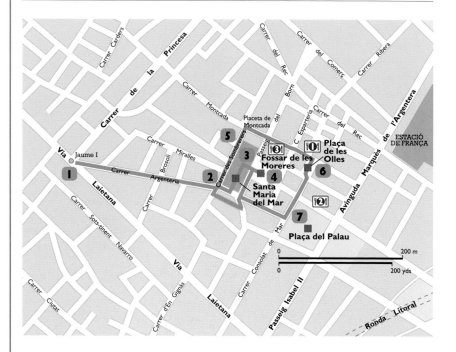

look for: the keystones, from front to back, represent the Coronation of the Virgin, the Nativity, the Annunciation, the equestrian figure of King Alfons III and the Barcelona coat of arms. The statue of Virgin and Child on the altar has a galleon at its base, a reminder of the basilica's maritime vocation. At the left rear of the church is a step where San Ignacio de Loyola, founder of the Jesuit Order, begged for alms in 1524 and 1525. The slabs in the floor are burial vaults for guilds, identified by a hat for the

hatters, or ships under sail for mariners. The stevedores who carried stones down from Montjuïc are honoured by the small bronze figures on the main door.

3 Leave the basilica by the sea-side middle door and walk out into the square beside the church with the low marble obelisk and the curved steel arch topped by the eternal flame.

The Fossar de les Moreres (Graveyard of the Mulberry Trees) commemorates

S.t JOSEP ORIOL   S.t IGNASI DE LOYOLA   S.t SALVADOR

the defeat of 11 September 1714, when Barcelona fell to the forces of Felipe V, the Bourbon pretender to the Spanish throne in the War of the Spanish Succession. This is a traditional rallying point for Catalan nationalists and fills with *catalanistas* every 11 September for La Diada, Catalonia's national day. The inscription reads: 'Here no traitor lies. Even losing our flag, this will be the urn of honour', a reference to the patriotic graveyard keeper who refused to bury a fallen Bourbon soldier here, even though it was his own son.

4 Walk back towards the front of the church, continue through Plaça de Santa Maria and Carrer de l'Anisadeta, go right on Carrer de les Caputxes, and then down the west side of Santa Maria del Mar to Casa Gispert.

The shops around Plaça de Santa Maria are noteworthy: the fashion store on the corner has a lovely 17th-century ceiling exposed during restoration. La Botifarreria de Santa Maria has a thousand varieties of hams and sausages. To the left of La Vinya de Senyor (The Lord's Vineyard), an excellent wine-tasting bar, is Carrer de l'Anisadeta, Barcelona's shortest street, measuring some 20ft (6m) from the corner to the edge of the square. To the right, Carrer de les Caputxes, named for the medieval makers of cowls or hoods, leaning under heavy timbers, is one of the Barri de la Ribera's most medieval spots. Cross Plaça de Santa Maria to Carrer dels Sombrerers, named for early hatters, and continue to Casa Gispert, one of Barcelona's oldest and most attractive stores, especially from

ABOVE: LA BOTIFARRERIA DE SANTA MARIA; OPPOSITE: CATALAN OLIVE OIL

the olfactory standpoint. The hazelnut roasting oven in the back of the store, the back door itself, the acid engravings on the glass office, and the aromas of nuts, teas, coffees, saffron, herbs and spices make Casa Gispert the fragrance capital of the city.

5 From Casa Gispert continue to the end of Carrer dels Sombrerers to the Placeta de Montcada and go right, crossing Passeig del Born and continuing through Carrer Vidrieria to Plaça de les Olles.

At Placeta de Montcada, take a look into the barred entrance to Carrer de les Mosques (Street of the Flies), Barcelona's narrowest street. Go right across Passeig del Born into Carrer Vidrieria, with the Atalanta textile print shop on the left and the Origens 99.9% restaurant, in what was previously a glass-blowing studio, to the right. Golfo de Bizkaia is a Basque tapas bar on the right, Custo Barcelona occupies the corner of Plaça de les Olles, and Cal Pep, a famous tapas restaurant, is at No. 8 at the end of the square.

6 After a look around Plaça de les Olles, walk out into Plaça del Palau to El Passadis del Pep.

Plaça de les Olles, named for pot (*olla*) makers (as in the Latin *olla podrida*, literally 'rotten pot' or stockpot), has several interesting buildings. Notice the apartment with colourful ceramic tiles under each balcony and on the top façade, and the Moderniste architect

Enric Sagnier i Villavecchia palace on the corner out to Plaça del Palau on the right with the conical turret jutting out over the street. Passadis del Pep is at the end of the passageway leading into the building at No. 2.

7 Turn left leaving Passadis del Pep and walk up Carrer Espaseria to Santa Maria del Mar.

The view from No. 2 Plaça del Palau up Carrer Espaseria, named for the makers of swords (*espadas*, for which Barcelona was famous in medieval times) is one of the classic vistas of the Santa Maria bell tower framed by the buildings on either side of the street. The walk ends here. Jaume I metro stop is a five-minute walk up Carrer Argenteria.

MUSICIANS PERFORM IN PLAÇA DE LES OLLES, LA RIBERA

Picasso and more at Born-Ribera

Barcelona's El Born has become synonymous with art, food, and fashion in an area once considered the heart of the city.

The Born, also known as Born-Ribera, centres around the Passeig del Born leading down to the Mercat del Born, at one time the city's main produce market. With shops and bars popping up like wild mushrooms, the Picasso Museum, and a fleet of new art galleries, this former Barcelona hub has made a major comeback over the last decade. *Roda al mon i torna al Born* was the time-honoured expression: 'Go around the world and come back to El Born'. Passeig del Born was the home of medieval jousting lists; the word *born* is Catalan for the business end of a lance, or perhaps the bitter end or edge of the city. Carrer Montcada was Barcelona's most aristocratic street in the 15th century, where noble families built Renaissance and baroque palaces with elegant patios, carriage ports and stairways. The Picasso Museum occupies five of these early palaces, which are nearly as interesting as the artworks they contain. The old Born market will soon become a city history museum.

From Jaume I metro stop or the intersection of Via Laietana and Carrer de la Princesa, walk up Via Laietana to Carrer de la Bòria and turn right. Walk through Plaça de la Llana and Carrer dels Corders to Placeta d'en Marcús and the Marcús chapel.

Carrer de la Bòria is the extension of Carrer Llibreteria across Via Laietana, part of the north-south artery present in all Rome's provincial cities. Plaça de la Llana, named for the wool (*llana*) market once held here, is a pungent, evocative square with all the dark and humid mystery of early Barcelona. Three streets open under arches into this little hub, which continues north as Carrer Corders (named for the makers of rope), down to the tiny 12th-century Marcús chapel, where medieval mail carriers, known as *els troters* (trotters), broke their journey in order to pray to the Virgen de la Guia, patron saint of travellers.

2 From Placeta Marcús, take Carrer Montcada across Carrer de la Princesa. Walk past the Picasso Museum to the bar El Xampanyet at No. 20.

Carrer Montcada was 13th-century Barcelona's most aristocratic street and is lined with elegant palaces built by noble families who were ceded the land by Sovereign Count-King Ramon Berenguer IV in 1148 after Guillem Ramón de Montcada organized and financed his victorious Tortosa campaign against the Moors. The Picasso Museum occupies the first five palaces, Palau

WHERE TO EAT

🍽 COMERÇ 24,
Carrer Comerç 24;
93-319-2102.
Creative and user-friendly gastronomic delights. €€€

🍽 PLA DE LA GARSA,
Carrer Assaonadors 13;
93-315-2413.
Diminutive maze of stairways and rooms with light fare. €€

🍽 TAVERNA DEL BORN,
Passeig del Born 27-29;
93-315-0964.
Sunny terrace and inside spaces serving tapas and light meals. €€

Aguilar, Palau Castellet, Palau Meca, Palau Mauri and Palau Finestres. With another annex in Plaça Sabartés presently being prepared, the Picasso Museum has prospered since its 1963 beginnings when, under the Franco dictatorship, Mayor Josep Maria Porcioles barely managed to allow the museum to open. Picasso spent his formative years in Barcelona between 1895 and 1904, and always felt a strong connection to the city even though he never set foot in Spain after the Franco victory in 1939. The museum is a stunning place to visit, meriting most of a morning, even though Picasso's best works are elsewhere.

3 Cross the street to the handsome patio of the Palau dels Marquesos

59

DISTANCE 1.3 miles (2.1km)

ALLOW 3 hours

START Capella d'en Marcús

FINISH Estació de França

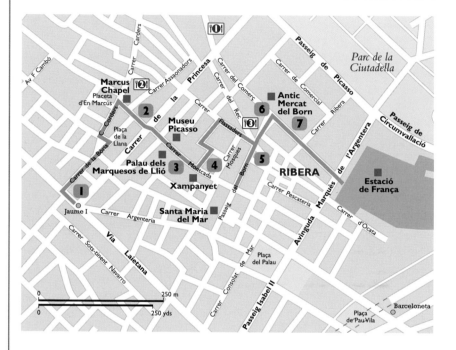

de Lló at No. 12 and then continue east on Carrer Montcada.

The Textile Café is an excellent place for a coffee or lunch in the sun. Further down Carrer Montcada, Palau Dalmases at No. 20 is notable for the baroque sculpted stairway in the elegant courtyard, portraying the Rape of Europe. Palau dels Cervelló at No. 25 is a 15th-century building with 16th-century detail and home of the Maeght Gallery. At No. 20 is the famous Xampanyet, a popular tavern known for its undrinkable sweet sparkling wine, to be avoided at all costs.

4 Across from El Xampanyet, duck into short, dark Carrer Arc de Sant Vicenç, and walk to the stone wall of La Seca, the early mint. Go left into Carrer de la Cirera and right out to Carrer dels Flassaders, before emerging to the right on Passeig del Born.

La Seca minted coins with the inscription *Principado de Cataluña* until 1836. Its

OPPOSITE: CARRER MONTCADA STREET LAMPS AND OLD BUILDINGS

OPPOSITE: CANNONBALL SCULPTURE UNDER PASSEIG DEL BORN BENCH

interior is an exquisitely restored split-level maze of wooden beams and pillars, the studio and showroom of sculptor Manel Álvarez. From the opening at the end of Arc de Sant Vicenç the chimney of the mint is overhead to the right. To the left at the corner of Carrer de la Cirera is the small, elevated chapel dedicated to Santa Maria de Cervelló, a protector of the Catalan fleet. Carrer dels Flassaders, named for medieval blanket-makers, is packed with boutiques and restaurants and worth exploration in both directions before walking out to the Born past the end of Carrer de les Mosques, where a carved stone face on the corner overhead marks the site of a former brothel.

5 Take a stroll up and down Passeig del Born. This slender and elongated square was where medieval jousts were held, along with markets, fairs, and Inquisitional *autos da fé*.

Passeig del Born, with Santa Maria del Mar to the south and the steel hangar Born market at the northern end, was once Barcelona's nerve centre. The bronze cannonballs and trunks refer to the area's destruction after the War of the Spanish Succession defeat in 1714, when 1000 houses, at the time about a third of the city, were demolished to create fields of fire for the occupying army in the Ciutadella. Bars and boutiques cluster along this popular street.

6 Walk to the north end of Passeig del Born to the steel hangar that houses Antic Mercat del Born.

Built in 1873 by Josep Fontseré, this steel structure was Barcelona's wholesale food market until the early 1970s. The fate of the Mercat del Born was uncertain until 2003 when the construction of a public library began on the site and the perfectly preserved remains of the 16th- and 17th-century neighbourhood, demolished and ploughed under by the military engineers of Felipe V, was discovered. The project was quickly snapped up by the City History Museum. Taverns, brothels, complete kitchens, houses shattered by cannonballs fired in the decisive 11 September 1714 battle, the canal that delivered water − everything is exactly as it was 300 years ago. The site is scheduled to become a museum with walkways through the early Born.

7 From the intersection of Passeig del Born with Carrer del Comerç, walk right to the Estació Barcelona de França across Av. Marquès de l'Argentera.

The Estació de França was Barcelona's main station until the mid-1980s, when Sants Station began to receive more and more train traffic. A 15-minute walk from Plaça Catalunya, a tapa in the Born, a drink in the bar car as the train left the curving steel hangar, and breakfast was on the table pulling into Paris Gare d'Austerlitz. Built in 1929 by architect Pedro Muguruza, the 12 tracks and seven platforms describe a graceful curve out to the left, while the materials and design all add up to quintessential old world railway terminus. The nearest metro stop is Barceloneta.

Fishermen, Gypsies, Seafood and Sand

Barceloneta, the fishermen's quarter, is a world apart, with a Bohemian, gypsy flair that makes the rest of Barcelona seem staid by comparison.

Barceloneta was open water until the mid-18th century when military engineers filled it in and began an urban housing project to compensate families from the Born area who had to tear their houses down after the 1714 siege. A traditional fishermen's quarter, where women could be seen repairing nets until the 1960s, there is still a fish auction every afternoon on the Moll dels Pescadors (Fishermen's Wharf). Laundry flapping from clothes lines over the streets gives Barceloneta a Neapolitan, romantic air, while dozens of restaurants and tapas bars do brisk business on Sundays and holidays. Since the restoration of the Barceloneta beach in the 1990s, the stretch of coast between the *escullera* (breakwater) and the Olympic Port has been full of young internationals soaking up the sun and even surfing. Since the 1992 Olympics, postmodern architect Frank Gehry's giant goldfish has added a contemporary touch to the Olympic Port end of the beach, but Barceloneta's salty charm has remained intact.

1 From the Barceloneta metro stop walk across the wide Carrer del Dr. Aiguader into Passeig Joan de Borbó Comte de Barcelona. From here, take the first street to the left, Carrer Balboa.

Crossing into Barceloneta, the Palau de Mar and the Catalan History Museum are off to the right across Plaça de Pau Vila. Carrer de Balboa takes you past a venerable tapas haunt, El Vaso de Oro at No. 6. Cut through Carrer Carbonell to Carrer de Ginebra, named for a 19th-century gin distillery that once operated here, and continue left past Lobito, with its awnings and outside tables on Passatge Carbonell. At the next corner is Bar Jai-Ca, another packed and friendly tapas-stacked tavern.

2 Cut right through Carrer Baluard and across Carrer Maquinista into the Plaça de la Font and the Mercat de la Barceloneta.

Can Ramonet, the flower-festooned pink house on the corner of Carrer Maquinista, is the oldest restaurant in Barceloneta. The newly restored Barceloneta market is always lively and filled with mouthwatering produce. The Lluçanès restaurant upstairs on the far side is an excellent place for lunch or dinner, while Els Fogons de la Barceloneta downstairs serves standard tapas and seafood. Plaça de la Font soon becomes Plaça del Poeta Boscà, a wide space with several more interesting bars around it, especially La Cova Fumada on the far right corner.

3 Cut right through Carrer Escuder and right again on Carrer Sant Miquel into Plaça de la Barceloneta.

Plaça de la Barceloneta is the home of the baroque Sant Miquel del Port church with its new St Michael Archangel statue in his undersized niche on the main façade. Destroyed during the Spanish Civil War (1936-39), St Michael's bright and buff replacement was erected in the 1980s. Look carefully for the small medallions or metopes adorning the façade, copies of the 74 gilt originals inside, each referring to the protection of St Michael against the perils of the sea. At No. 41 Carrer de Sant Miquel is a plaque to Fernando de Lesseps (1805-1984), engineer of the Panama and Suez canals, who lived here as French consul to Barcelona. Can Ganassa to the right is a worthy tapas bar.

4 Walk east one block on Carrer Sant Elm to reach the corner of Carrer Sant Carles.

The house at No. 6 Carrer Sant Carles is the last original two-storey, 1755 Barceloneta house left standing. The military engineers who built Barceloneta allowed only two storeys so as not to mask the sound of the Ciutadella cannon guarding the port. Planned as single-family dwellings, with shop and storage space on the ground floor and living space above, houses were soon subdivided and overcrowded. In the mid-19th century, after over a century of Madrid-based military rule, homeowners finally

DISTANCE 1.6 miles (2.4km)

ALLOW 3 hours

START Barceloneta metro station

FINISH Ciutadella-Vila Olímpica metro station

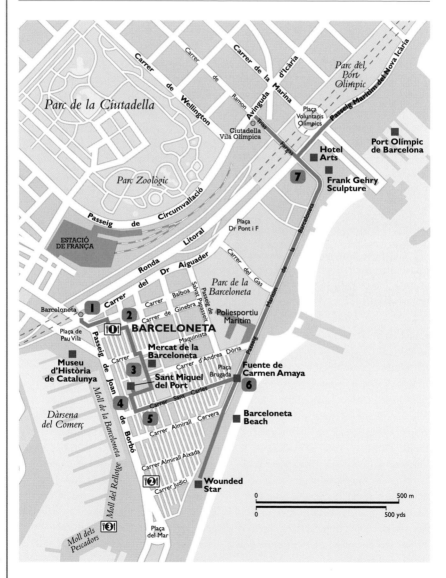

gained permission to build higher. The ornate house at No. 7 with floral trim around the upper balconies, griffins over the door, and the pharmacist's insignia (serpent and amphora) is Farmacia Saim, Barceloneta's first pharmacy. The present house, built in 1902, was used as a bomb shelter during the Spanish Civil War (1936-39) when Franco's bombers, attempting to paralyze the port, dumped bombs on Barceloneta. The Moderniste building on the corner of Carrer de Santa Clara is the Cooperative Obrera La Fraternitat (Brotherhood Workers' Cooperative), the only Art Nouveau building in Barceloneta. Begun in 1879 as an outlet to help supply workers with basic necessities at cut-rate prices, the cooperative eventually became a social and cultural centre and library.

67

ABOVE: THE REBECCA HORN SCULPTURE *WOUNDED STAR*

WHERE TO EAT

🍴 LOBITO,
Carrer Ginebra 9;
93-319-9164.
Fresh fish and seafood explode forth
from the kitchen. €€€

🍴 SUQUET DEL ALMIRALL,
Passeig Joan de Borbó 65;
93-221-6233.
Intimate terrace and dining room
serving great fish and seafood. €€€

🍴 BARCELONETA,
Escar 22;
93-221-2111.
A vast and rollicking dining room
serving rice and seafood specialities.
€€

5 Continue down Carrer Sant Carles to the Carmen Amaya monument at the end of the street, where it intersects with Passeig Marítim de la Barceloneta.

Carrer Sant Carles continues east past a series of interesting buildings, all the way to the Fuente de Carmen Amaya (Carmen Amaya Fountain) at the end of the street. The monument honours the famous flamenco dancer Carmen Amaya (1913-63), born in the gypsy community of Somorrostro that was part of Barceloneta until 1920. Amaya achieved fame at the age of 16, performing at Barcelona's International Exposition in 1929 and made triumphal tours of the Americas, starring in films such as

La hija de Juan Simón (1934) and *Los Tarantos* (1962). The fountain, populated with cherubs dancing flamenco, recalls Barceloneta's history as a free-wheeling, romantic enclave of sailors, gypsies, and fishermen. The gypsies all but disappeared when the *chiringuitos* (beach shacks serving fish and rice dishes) were demolished after the 1992 Olympics.

6 Walk to the right for a look at the Barceloneta beach and restaurants.

The Barceloneta beach is, in summer, an international fiesta. The Can Majó terrace restaurant at the end of Carrer Almirall Aixada is one of the best for rice and fish. The Rebecca Horn sculpture *Wounded*

ABOVE: FRANK GEHRY'S GOLDFISH SCULPTURE

Star, an irregular leaning tower of rusting cubes, seems to pay homage to the historic demolished *chiringuitos*.

7 Walk back east to the Frank Gehry goldfish sculpture and the Hotel Arts before having a look through the Olympic Port. Then head west to the Ciutadella-Vila Olímpica metro station.

From Passeig Marítim de la Barceloneta the Moderniste Torre de les Aïgues (water tower) is visible off to the left. The nearby Torre del Gas Natural, officially entitled Torre Mare Nostrum ('Our Sea', in Latin, as the Mediterranean is affectionately dubbed by Catalans) by the late Enric Miralles (1955-2000), architect of the Santa Caterina market, offers a gleaming glass and titanium contrast. Hospital de Mar, another contemporary architectural star, was much photographed in Pedro Almodovar's 1999 film *All About My Mother*. Around the skyscraper Hotel Arts are designer clubs and restaurants: the Carpe Diem Lounge Club, Shoko, Baja Beach Club, and the Agua and Bestial restaurants, all hot destinations for seekers of contemporary design and postmodern excitement. The clubs and restaurants along the quay in the Olympic Port are uniformly noisy and overpopulated. The nearest metro stop is Ciutadella-Vila Olímpica station, which can deliver you to Plaça Urquinaona, next to Plaça Catalunya, in five minutes.

69

Lower Gothic Quarter

The seamy lower edge of the Gothic Quarter holds some surprising treasures, assorted tapas dives and an under-the-radar art collection.

Between Plaça Reial and La Llotja de Mar, Barcelona's medieval maritime exchange, once home of the city's main art school, there are pungent undiscovered corners. From Plaça Reial's dodgy neoclassical formality teetering on the edge of Mediterranean mayhem, through the improving but still seedy Carrer Escudellers into the relatively recently opened Plaça de George Orwell, keep your wits, and your valuables, about you. The cobblestone alleyway down to the Basilica de la Mercé has long been a favourite promenade for those intrepid enough to find it, with Our Lady of Mercy gleaming in the sun atop her basilica at the end of the street. Carrer Ample is lined with shops and restaurants in both directions, while the next street towards the port, Carrer de la Mercé, was the city's one and only tapas crawl until late in the 20th century. Across Via Laietana, the Gothic Llotja de Mar hiding behind its neoclassical façade conceals the art school where Picasso and Gaudí studied, as well as the seldom seen Reial Acadèmia de Belles Arts de Sant Jordi art collection.

From the Liceu metro stop on the Rambla, walk through Plaça Reial and out the far righthand corner. Turn left on Carrer dels Escudellers at the roasting chickens outside Los Caracoles. Continue walking ahead to Plaça de George Orwell.

Carrer Escudellers was the northern annex of the Raval's famous Barrio Chino flesh market as late as the 1980s, with ranks of painted women for sale and the US 6th Fleet all too happy to stimulate the economy. The area has improved (or deteriorated, depending on your point of view) since then, but it's still far from squeaky clean. After rows of bars, inebriates, and offbeat personages of all kinds, Plaça George Orwell, which did not exist until 1990, opens to the surrealist sculpture entitled, simply, *Monument* by Catalan sculptor Leandre Cristòfol (1908-99). There is no known relationship between the sculpture and George Orwell (1903-50), although the surveillance camera in the square is very Big Brother. The plaque to Orwell is on the far side of the square. Dubbed 'Plaza Trippy', a reference to the psychedelic substances consumed by the numerous youths who gather here to share litre bottles of Xibeca beer and anything else being passed around, Plaça Orwell seems faint homage for the author of *Homage to Catalonia*, though Orwell's experiences in Barcelona during the Spanish Civil War (1936-39) were nothing if not surreal and psychedelic. Shot through the throat with no serious damage while serving at the front in Aragón, Orwell was subsequently placed on a hit list as a Trotskyite for having served with the anarchist Partido Obrero Unificado Marxista (POUM) militia, before barely escaping the country with his life. Most Orwellian scholars consider *Animal Farm* and his break with Marxism a direct result of his experiences in the defence of Republican Spain.

2 Take the only street to the right out of Plaça George Orwell, Carrer d'en Carabassa, and continue straight on to the end of the street to the Basilica of La Mercé.

This quirky cobbled street with tiny bridges connecting what were once palatial townhouses with their back

WHERE TO EAT

🍴 AGUT,
Carrer Gignàs 16;
93-315-1709.
A simple family-run operation serving top value Catalan cuisine. €

🍴 REIAL CLUB NAÚTIC DE BARCELONA,
Moll d'Espanya 2-3;
93-221-6508.
Rice dishes and seafood served in Barcelona's yacht club in the port. €€

🍴 CLÀSSIC GÒTIC,
Carrer de la Plata 3;
93-319-9298.
Classical Catalan cuisine in Pablo Picasso's first studio. €€

10

DISTANCE 1.2 miles (1.9km)

ALLOW 2.5 hours

START Liceu metro station

FINISH Jaume I metro station

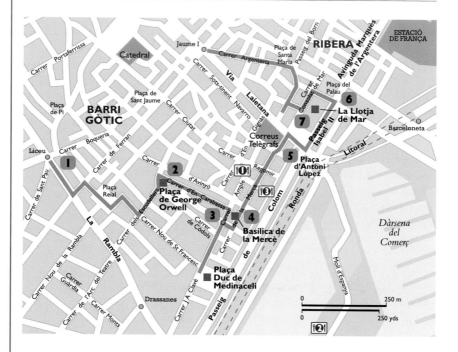

gardens has long been a favourite of artists and the soft urban underbelly of organized life. When a project to demolish these ancient structures in favour of more profitable modern buildings was approved a decade ago, social outrage ended up derailing the proposal. Our Lady of Mercy atop her basilica, especially when illuminated by the afternoon sun, looms impossibly huge at the end of the street. Just before reaching the first bridge, look for the Bacchic *sgraffito* (see page 32) designs

overhead to the left, some of the best in Barcelona for their grace and subtlety. At the end of the street on the lateral façade of the baroque Basilica de la Mercé is a curious Gothic doorway upon which St Michael is sculpted delivering a perfect squash backhand (with, alas, a sword) to the Lucifer at his feet. This door was taken from the Sant Miquel chapel that once stood just off Plaça Sant Jaume next to the Town Hall after it was torn down to make space for more municipal offices. The grocery store, La

Leonesa, on the corner of Carrer Ample, has one of Barcelona's best original 19th-century shopfronts.

3 Turn right onto Carrer Ample and go down to Plaça Duc de Medinaceli and back to Plaça de la Mercé.

A walk to the right down Carrer Ample leads to Plaça Duc de Medinaceli, a charming square used by Pedro Almodovar in his 1999 film *All About My Mother*. Le Tre Venezie at No. 4 is an excellent Italian restaurant. The store Solé at No. 7 Carrer Ample sells handmade shoes from around the world. Back in Plaça de la Mercé, the large building on the sea side of the square was once the military headquarters governing Barcelona during the 1939-75 Franco regime. The Capitanía General is still quartered here. The Basilica de la Mercé, with the exception of the La Mercé herself and the Gothic Sant Miquel door, is of little architectural interest.

4 Leave the Basilica de la Mercé to your left and start down Carrer de la Mercé, continuing to Correus, the post office, at the end of the street.

Believe it or not, in a city now gone tapas-happy, this was Barcelona's only tapas crawl as late as 1980. Tapas, always a custom of Spain, originally from Andalucía, only caught on in Barcelona when commercially astute Catalans finally figured out that tapas and tourists added up to big business. All of the bars and *tascas* along Carrer de la Mercé

ABOVE: THE BAROQUE FAÇADE OF LA MERCÉ

serve different delicacies, ranging from Bar Celta, the Galician *pulpo* (squid) specialist at the corner of Carrer Simó Oller, to Bar de la Plata's little fried fish at the corner of Carrer de la Plata. The restaurant Clàssic Gòtic is just to the left in the building with the plaque attesting to the Picasso studio that it once housed.

5 From the end of Carrer de la Mercé and the main city post office, continue across Via Laietana, walk to the right through the square to Passeig d'Isabel II, and continue to La Llotja de Mar at No. 3.

From the square in front of the post office the yacht marina is visible across Passeig de Colom behind the Lichtenstein *Barcelona Head* sculpture. At the door into La Llotja, unless things change, visitors are only allowed up into the Reial Acadèmia de Belles Arts de Sant Jordi. Ask for the museum or the Acadèmia and the receptionists will send you to the elevator. The curators of the art museum are overjoyed to have visitors, as the museum is as yet not an official art venue and has no budget for monitors or receptionists. The best works in the museum are the Marià Fortuny (1838–74) drawings of burly Romans from his fellowship year in Rome in 1858. Fortuny's most famous painting is the huge *Battle of Tetuán* canvas he did on commission for the Spanish government during Spain's colonial war in Morocco. The Llotja art school was Barcelona's main art academy, where Picasso's father taught and where the 15-year-old Picasso

was briefly enrolled when he first moved to Barcelona in 1895. La Llotja's Gothic Hall is one of Barcelona's finest Gothic treasures and well worth bribing a guard to have a look into, but at the time of writing it was still not open to the public.

6 Walk left around the end of La Llotja de Mar and then go left again on Carrer Consolat de Mar to the first possible right under porches supporting medieval buildings.

This is another one of Barcelona's marvellously medieval corners. Notice the wood-beamed apartments overhead. One of them is rumoured to have briefly housed the Ruiz-Picasso family in 1895 when the artist's father was teaching at La Llotja art school, opposite. Across the street, don't miss the neoclassical façade covering the Gothic Hall, added during Barcelona's blessedly brief mid-18th century passion for straight lines.

7 Walk through Carrer Trompetes into Carrer dels Agullers. Turn left up to Vila Viniteca before turning back down Carrer Agullers to the corner of Carrer Canvis Vells, where a left turn will take you into Plaça de Santa Maria.

Vila Viniteca, Barcelona's best wine store, is worth a browse, as is the delicatessen across the street specializing in cheeses from all over Europe. On Carrer Canvis Vells, on the right is Baraka, the city's foremost Moroccan store and general cultural centre. The Jaume I metro stop is five minutes up Carrer Argenteria.

Upper Raval: Art, music, shops and skateboarding

Originally a slum outside the walls that ran down the eastern side of the Rambla, this global community centres on a dazzling art museum.

Derived from the Spanish word *arrabal* meaning outskirts or slum, the Barcelona Raval, west of the Rambla, has until recently been known as a place of illicit activities ranging from prostitution to drug dealing. The upper Raval, taken as the area above Carrer del Carme, continuing across Carrer de Sant Antoni Abat, and bordered to the west by Ronda de Sant Antoni and to the north by Carrer Pelai, changed with the addition of the Richard Meier contemporary art museum (MACBA), an eruption of space, white planes, glass, and light, becoming nearly completely gentrified into a cultural and shopping area with galleries, university classrooms, boutiques, hotels and restaurants. The Centre de Cultura Contemporania de Barcelona (CCCB) and the Foment dels Arts Decoratives i de Disseny (FAD) in the Convent dels Àngels have further made the upper Raval an oasis of culture informed by a resident community dominated by immigrants from countries around the Mediterranean and beyond.

1 From Plaça Catalunya's Bar Zurich, start down the Rambla and take the first right into Carrer Tallers. Continue down Carrer Tallers to the corner of Carrer Valldonzella and turn left.

Carrer Tallers, named for the medieval butchers (*tallar* means 'to cut' in Catalan) who worked here, is a bustling artery filled with young people walking to and from the new university buildings around the MACBA and shopping for music and concert tickets. Carrer Tallers is the city's main music street, with numerous music stores such as Revolver and Discos Castelló with vast recording selections, as well as sales of tickets to pop concerts of all kinds. The first street off to the left, Carrer de les Sitges, leads down to the cave-like student beer bar L'Ovella Negra (The Black Sheep), a throwback to the medieval university's tenure here, before Felipe V had the students exiled to Cervera, 62 miles (100km) west of Barcelona, in 1715.

2 From the corner of Carrer Valldonzella and Tallers, walk left to Carrer Montalegre and take another left down to the CCCB and the MACBA.

First on the right at No. 7 is the entrance to Casa de la Caritat-Pati Manning, an orphanage and a seminary until 1956 and since 1994 a cultural resource run by Centre d'Estudi i Recerca Cultural (CERC). The next entrance is the Centre de Cultura Contemporania de Barcelona (CCCB), also originally part of the Casa de la Caritat, and now a venue for

WHERE TO EAT

|O| MAM I TECA,
Carrer Lluna 4;
93-441-3335.
Just a few tables but very well supplied with local fare. €€

|2| CENTRO RIOJANO DE BARCELONA,
Carrer Peu de la Creu 8-10;
93-443-3363.
Home cooking from Spain's La Rioja wine country. €€

|3| ÈS,
Doctor Dou 14;
93-301-0068.
A contemporary space serving light Mediterranean food to match. €€

art exhibitions, lectures and concerts. Architects Helio Piñón and Albert Viaplana placed a dark glass façade on the right side of the courtyard that reflects Montjuïc and the Mediterranean, another notable combination of contemporary design and traditional architecture. Occupying the corner of Plaça dels Àngels is the MACBA, the contemporary art museum that is most responsible for Raval's modern recovery. Richard Meier's 1995 cylindrical three-storey reception hall subdivides the cubic structure, while ramps leading to the exhibition floor crisscross the inside of the glass façade. Permanent exhibits include works by artists such as Calder, Rauschenberg, Oteiza and Chillida.

OPPOSITE: MUSEU D'ART CONTEMPORANI DE BARCELONA (MACBA)

11

DISTANCE 1.5 miles (2.3km)

ALLOW 3 hours

START Plaça Catalunya metro station

FINISH Sant Antoni metro station

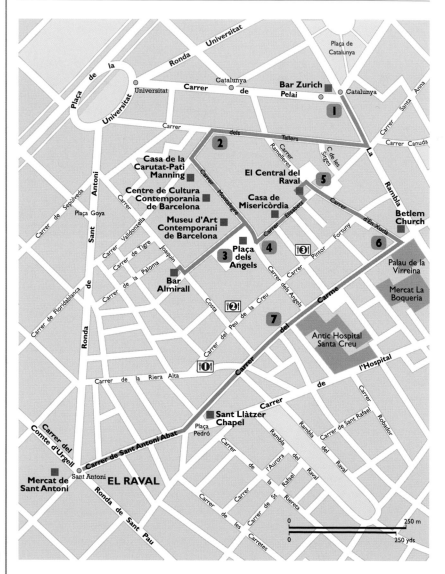

3 Walk around Plaça dels Àngels and across Carrer Joaquín Costa to the Moderniste Bar Almirall before walking back through the square and the Convent dels Àngels.

Basque sculptor Jorge Oteiza's (1908-2003) massive bronze *La Ola (The Wave)* on the MACBA front porch is popular with skateboarders comparing skills in dozens of languages from Arabic to Pakistani, while Eduardo Chillida's *Barcelona*, a blocky black puzzle, adorns the wall behind the terrace café just beyond the museum. Carrer Ferlandina leads out to the right of the entrance. On the far corner of Carrer Joaquin Costa is Bar Almirall, one of the best Moderniste bars in town, while a few steps further on is Horiginal Café & Poesia Restaurant, with terrace, dining and occasional jazz

at Ferlandina 29. Back in Plaça dels Àngels, Foment dels Arts Decoratives i de Disseny (FAD) shows contemporary design in the 16th-century convent.

4 Walk back east on Carrer d'Elisabets to the bookstore El Central del Raval and walk through this former chapel, emerging on Carrer de les Ramelleres.

Carrer d'Elisabets leads back towards the Rambla past the Hotel Camper. Several interesting boutiques, studios and galleries are on the left side of Carrer del Doctor Dou, the first street to the right. The towering palm tree and the ivy-covered walls are the Casa de la Misericordia, originally associated with the Casa de la Caritat before the male and female sections of the orphanage were separated.

79

ABOVE: RAVAL (MACBA) CAFÉ WITH EDUARDO CHILLIDA'S *BARCELONA* BEHIND

II

The Casa de la Misericordia chapel at No. 6 has a wonderful collection of books under a vaulted ceiling. The bookstore leads back through to its restaurant and eventually out to Carrer de les Ramelleres, running beside Plaça de Vicenç Martorell. Here, look for *el torn*, the wooden turntable in the wall just to the right of No. 17, on which foundlings and abandoned infants were passed to the nuns of the Casa de la Misericordia.

5 Walk across Carrer d'Elisabets and the edge of leafy Plaça del Bonsuccés into Carrer d'en Xuclà, the continuation of Carrer de les Ramelleres, and continue down to the corner of Carrer del Carme.

Carrer d'en Xuclà leads past the Herboristeria Guarro on the right at No. 23, always a good stop for a breath of sweet herbal air. On the corner of Carrer del Pintor Fortuny is a marble statue of Marià Fortuny (1838-74) – Spain's most important 19th-century painter after Goya – who drew the burly Romans at La Llotja in Walk 10. Farther along, at No. 5, is an oddity in a city that has declared itself an enemy of bullfighting; the restaurant and taurine club Los de Gallito y de Belmonte, with a good selection of tapas and bullfighting photographs and memorabilia. The corner of Carrer del Carme brings a chance to have a close look at the sculpted figures on the façade of the Betlem church.

6 Walk down Carrer del Carme to Bar Muy Buenas at No. 63.

Across the street, Xocolater Bellart at No. 3 Carrer del Carme is an artisan chocolate shop. The ceiling painting and rich Moderniste woodworking date from the store's 1890 founding. El Indio at No. 24 is an old-fashioned textile house with lengthy wooden cutting tables. Art Nouveau details include acid engravings in the glass and parabolic hyperboloid-shaped door handles. (The parabolic hyperboloid, Gaudí's most characteristic arch, shaped like the web of skin between your fingers, is made by hanging a chain from two points. It's also known as the catenary arch.) Bar Muy Buenas, down Carrer del Carme, is a gorgeous bar with looping wooden Moderniste décor.

7 Continue through Carrer del Carme past Plaça del Pedró into Carrer de Sant Antoni Abat to the Mercat de Sant Antoni and the Sant Antoni metro station.

The walk out to the Ronda de Sant Antoni leads past the pre-Romanesque Sant Llàtzer chapel, the medieval leper's chapel, with a detour left into Carrer de Sant Llàtzer to see the apse. The front of the chapel looks out on Plaça del Pedró, where the Santa Eulàlia monument marks the spot where the saint was crucified on an X-shaped cross in the 4th century. Straight out Carrer de Sant Antoni is the Sant Antoni market, a gorgeous steel hangar now in partial use as a food market and better known as a weekend flea market for second-hand clothing and books. The Sant Antoni metro station is on the corner.

OPPOSITE: BETLEM CHURCH ARCHANGEL MICHAEL

Lower Raval: Sex, drugs and rock & roll

The notorious Barrio Chino spreads out in the lower Raval from Carrer Hospital down to Drassanes shipyards. The area is known for its nightlife.

Barcelona's Barrio Chino, for years more emblematic of the city than Gaudí, has raged unchecked and unrepentant for centuries. Picasso's paintings of circus acrobats and gypsies were inspired by the same prostitutes, transvestites, pimps, gypsies, scam artists, drug dealers and common thieves that inspired French novelist Jean Genet (1910-86) as well as numerous other writers, from surrealist Pieyre de Mandiargues (1909-91) to recent phenomenon Carlos Ruiz Zafón, author of worldwide bestselling *The Shadow of the Wind* (2001). Though all of the Raval is sometimes called the Barrio Chino (Barri Xinès in Catalan, but generally known as the Barrio Chino), the authentic 'Chino' is, fittingly, between Plaça de Jean Genet and Plaça de Salvador Seguí in the heart of the neighbourhood. With Gaudí's Moderniste Palau Güell and Barcelona's earliest Christian church, Sant Pau del Camp, as bookends, and the Rambla del Raval as central runway, there is much to see in this colourful slice of the real Barcelona.

From the Liceu metro station, walk two blocks down the Rambla to the corner of Carrer Nou de la Rambla. Turn right to Palau Güell at No. 9.

Palau Güell was Gaudí's first commission from Count Eusebi Güell (1846-1918), the man who would become his main patron. The town house opened in 1888 for the World Exhibition, with Princesses Paz and Isabel de Borbón, daughters of King Alfonso XII, attending the inaugural gala. In the basement stables are a series of mushroom-like columns that support the building. The chutes on the street side of the stables were for delivering feed for the horses, while the spiral ramp was the servants' access. The pine-block flooring on the ground-floor entranceway was designed to deaden the sound of horses' hoofs. Prisoners were held here during the Spanish Civil War (1936-39), when the stables were used as a *cheka* or Stalinist secret-police dungeon. The most famous prisoner was Andreu Nin (1892-1937), a purged Trotskyite who was never seen again. On the main floor, the third reception room, with its intricately coffered ceiling, has a latticed jalousie, a double screen through which Count Güell was able to eavesdrop on his visitors. The central atrium, a three-story parabolic cupola reaching up above the roofline, was the grand hall used for parties, receptions and musical evenings. Musicians played from the balcony, with the overhead window reserved for the soloist. A fold-out chapel of beaten copper with retractable kneeling pads and a small two-seater bench built into the right side of the altar is enclosed behind a double door, with a small organ with pipes climbing the central gallery. The dining room's Art Nouveau fireplace, in the shape of a horseshoe arch, is next to a mahogany table seating 10. Polished grey marble walls from Count Güell's quarry in El Garraf are visible from outside on the porch. Brick servants' quarters rise up on the left, while a passageway out towards the Rambla linked Palau Güell with the Count's father's house. The upstairs bedrooms of Count Güell and his wife, Isabel López, have built-in wardrobes padded in lilac velvet with their initials intertwined in wrought-iron. The bathroom is equipped with all the modern conveniences… of 1888. But the roof is where we find the playful Gaudí of Park Güell. The chimneys are kaleidoscopic, the main one crowned by a bat weathervane, the favourite emblem of King Jaume I el Conqueridor.

OPPOSITE: KALEIDOSCOPIC CHIMNEYS AT PALAU GÜELL; ABOVE: WROUGHT IRON ON THE FAÇADE

DISTANCE **1.3 miles (2.2km)**

ALLOW **2 hours**

START **Liceu metro station**

FINISH **El Paral.lel metro station**

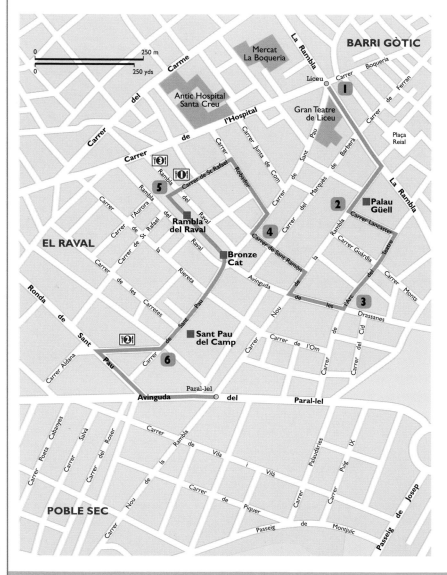

OPPOSITE: TRENCADIS MOSAIC ATOP GAUDÍ'S PALAU GÜELL

WHERE TO EAT

🍴 CASA LEOPOLDO,
Carrer Sant Rafael 24;
93-241-3014.
The Raval's "clean, well lighted place",
with excellent seafood. €€

🍴 CA L'ISIDRE,
Carrer de les Flors 12;
93-441-1139.
Considered by cognoscenti to be
Barcelona's hautest haute cuisine. €€

🍴 LA REINA DEL RAVAL,
Rambla del Raval 3;
93-443-3655.
Contemporary décor and creative
Mediterranean fare. €€€

2 Continue down Carrer Nou de la Rambla, taking the first left on Carrer Lancaster. At the end of the street turn right on Carrer de l'Arc del Teatre and walk all the way to the end, to Plaça de Jean Genet.

Carrer Lancaster is the home of two Raval institutions: Bar Bohemia, where cabaret has been belted out since 1893, and the croissant factory, where Barcelona night owls line up for hot croissants on the way home in the wee hours. Around the corner on Carrer de l'Arc del Teatre is Bar Pastis, serving the French aniseed drink and playing non-stop Edith Piaf. Continue to the end of the street to Plaça Jean Genet for a quick look at the drag queen headquarters.

3 From Plaça de Jean Genet, walk to the right up Avinguda de les Drassanes to Carrer Nou de la Rambla, go right and then left into Carrer de Sant Ramón, two blocks up past Plaça de Pieyre de Mandiargues to the corner of Carrer de Sant Pau.

These streets are where French author Jean Genet (1910-86) spent his early 20s gathering material that would eventually be published as *The Thief's Journal* in 1949. Peyre de Mandiargues, the French surrealist, published *La Marge*, set in the feverish streets of the Raval, in 1967. At the corner of Carrer de Sant Ramón and Carrer de Sant Pau is the Bar Marsella, unchanged since Dalí and Picasso quaffed absinthe here in the 1920s.

4 Go right on Carrer de Sant Pau for a few steps and then take the first left into Carrer d'en Robador. Walk up Carrer d'en Robador past the eponymous jazz bar at No. 55 and take a left on Carrer de Sant Rafael over to the Rambla del Raval.

Casa Leopoldo is at Sant Rafael 24, and, once out on the Rambla del Raval, the Reina del Raval restaurant is near the top of the street on the right. Left down Rambla del Raval is the Fernando Botero bronze sculpture of an elephantine cat, near the corner of Carrer de Sant Pau.

5 Walk right on Carrer de Sant Pau. Stop at the entrance to the Sant Pau del Camp church near the end of the street.

Barcelona's oldest church was originally *del camp* or 'in the fields' outside the second set of city walls. Though archaeological evidence points to an earlier church and cemetery on the same spot, what you see now was built in 1127 and is the earliest Romanesque architecture in Barcelona. Elements of the church (the classical marble capitals atop the columns in the main entry) are thought to be from the 6th and 7th centuries or recycled Roman ruins. The hulking shape of the church reflects Christianity's defensive crouch in the face of 10th-century Moorish attacks. The church is acoustically perfect and musical performances here are not to be missed. The tiny stained-glass window high on the façade facing Carrer Sant Pau is probably the world's smallest. The intimate cloister, with carved capitals portraying biblical scenes supporting triple Mudéjar arches, is Sant Pau del Camp's finest feature.

6 Walk across Carrer de Sant Pau, into Carrer de les Flors. Go past Ca l'Isidre restaurant and take a left at the corner of Ronda de Sant Antoni to Avinguda del Paral.lel.

The Paral.lel is Barcelona's Broadway, and theatres are everywhere. Nou Tantarantana, just past Ca l'Isidre, stages avant-garde shows. Directly across the street is El Molino, the city's Moulin Rouge chorus line venue for most of the 20th century. Teatre Victoria is at the end of the next block across to the left; the Teatre Apolo is a vibrant disco. The Paral.lel metro stop takes you back to the top of the Rambla in five minutes.

ABOVE: FERNANDO BOTERO'S BRONZE CAT SCULPTURE

SANT PAU DEL CAMP CHURCH

Central Eixample

The Eixample was built at a moment of economic power and quickly filled with Art Nouveau architecture and elegant townhouses.

After years of petitioning Madrid and the military authorities for permission to tear down the city walls that had ringed the Ciutat Vella (Old City) since the 13th century, deteriorating health conditions in the overpopulated city centre finally convinced central government that the time had come. The area between the city walls and the outlying towns Sants, Sarrià, Gràcia and Horta, a barren no-man's land, was soon replaced by the immense chequerboard Eixample (Expansion) conceived by city planner Ildefons Cerdà (1815-76). A living museum of Moderniste architecture and the commercial and business centre of the city, the Eixample is both avant-garde and urbane. Unofficially divided into the Esquerra (left) and Dreta (right), once considered representative of, respectively, the working class and the bourgeoisie, the traditional dividing line was Carrer Balmes, then the Sarrià railway tracks, placing the Eixample's two main arteries, Rambla de Catalunya and Passeig de Gràcia, in the Dreta.

From the Diagonal metro station walk through the Palau Robert and across Carrer Còrsega to the top of Rambla Catalunya at Avinguda Diagonal.

Palau Robert, an elegant palace with a concert hall, is also the Turisme de Catalunya information point, with maps, pamphlets and materials for those who wish to organize trips outside town. At the top of Rambla Catalunya, don't miss the clownishly reclining bronze giraffe, *Coqueta* (Flirt), sculpted by Josep Granyer (1899-1983) and placed here in 1972. To the left looking down Rambla Catalunya is Casa Serra, built in 1907 by Josep Puig i Cadafalch (1867-1956), the most prolific and politically important but, curiously, least known of the top trio of Moderniste architects that included Antoni Gaudí (1852-1926) and Lluís Domènech i Montaner (1850-1923).

PALAU ROBERT;

www.gencat.cat/palaurobert

2 Start down Rambla de Catalunya and walk left through Passatge de Concepció to Passeig de Gràcia and across to the design store Vinçon.

There are 45 of these alleys or passageways (*passatges*) through the blocks of Cerdà's grid, each of them distinct and intimate. Passatge de la Concepció is a favourite for its restaurants. Sculptor Lorenzo Quinn, son of movie star Anthony Quinn, owns and runs Pòsit Galeria Gastronómica at No. 7. Tragaluz at No. 5 is a design hotspot, while El Japonés across the street at No. 2 serves

WHERE TO EAT

[O] **TAPAÇ 24,**
Carrer Diputació 269;
93-488-0977.
Tapas and light meals with flair in the mid-Eixample. €€

[O] **DROLMA,**
Passeig de Gràcia 68;
93-496-7710.
Classic Mediterranean cuisine by one of Catalonia's master chefs, Fermin Puig. €€€

[O] **CIUDAD CONDAL,**
Rambla de Catalunya 18;
93-318-1997.
Bounty on the bar or à table, either tapas or full meals. €

some of the city's best Japanese food in a sleek contemporary setting designed by Isabel López and Sandra Tarruella, two very busy young interior designers. Across Passeig de Gràcia at No. 96 is the Vinçon design store, Barcelona's most famous, with knick-knacks and design items of every size and price in a Moderniste palace that was once the home of the painter Santiago Rusiñol (1861-1931).

VINÇON DESIGN STORE;

www.vincon.com

3 Walk down Passeig de Gràcia to the corner of Carrer de Provença where Antoni Gaudí's Casa Milà, popularly known as La Pedrera, undulates around the corner.

DISTANCE **2 miles (3.2km)**

ALLOW **3 hours**

START **Diagonal metro station**

FINISH **Plaça de Catalunya metro station**

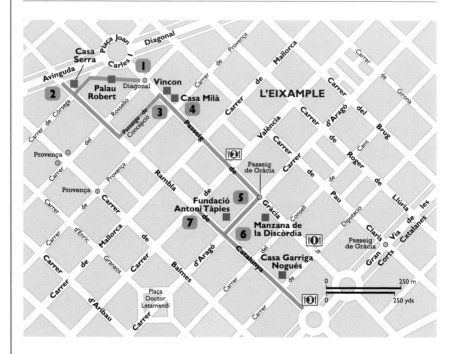

La Pedrera means 'the quarry' in Catalan, a not-so-complimentary nickname the building acquired soon after it was unveiled in 1905. The Milà family, who had never been fully aware of exactly how the building was going to look, was reportedly horrified when the tarpaulins were removed; Sra. Milà was quoted as saying that it looked like a place for 'snakes and wild animals'. The art gallery on the first floor houses temporary exhibits. Upstairs is the Espai Gaudí museum in the attic, the rooftop and iconic chimney caps, and a 19th-century apartment that is maintained with period furnishings and gadgets.

LA PEDRERA;

www.lapedreraeducacio.org

4 Continue down Passeig de Gràcia for three blocks to reach Carrer d'Aragó. Cross over to the far side for a look at the famous Manzana de la Discòrdia or Apple/Block of Discord, where the three leading Moderniste architects worked alongside each other.

ABOVE: INTERIOR OF GAUDÍ'S CASA MILÀ OR LA PEDRERA

These façades were added to existing buildings in the first five years of the 20th century. After viewing them from a distance, cross Passeig de Gràcia for a closer look at the three buildings. Gaudí's Casa Batlló is on the right, with the scaly roof and the colourful façade. The roof is meant to evoke the dragon of the St George and dragon legend, a theme much repeated in Catalonia, where Sant Jordi is the local patron saint. Its interior is even more dazzling, with Jules Verne underwater themes swirling over walls and ceilings. To the left, at No. 41, is Puig i Cadafalch's Casa Amatller, an eclectic or historicist Netherlands-style façade richly sculpted by Eusebi Arnau (1863-1933), a leading Moderniste sculptor. The barely Moderniste Casa Mulleras at No. 37 is by architect Enric Sagnier i Villavecchia (1858-1931). The last Moderniste façade is on the corner of Carrer Consell de Cent, Lluís Domènech i Montaner's Casa Lleó Morera, over the Loewe store, with sculptures on the façade depicting turn-

of-the-20th-century modern inventions such as the camera and the telephone. The interior, with stunning Eusebi Arnau sculptures and colourful murals is, at the time of writing, closed to the public.

CASA BATLLÓ;

www.casabatllo.es

CASA AMATLLER;

www.amatller.org

5 Next walk back up to Carrer d'Aragó and turn left. Across the street you will see Casa Montaner i Simó, now the Fundació Tàpies.

Originally a publishing house, this Lluís Domènech i Montaner building was the first Moderniste building in the Eixample, built in 1880. The tangle of wire on the roof, entitled *Núvol i cadira* (*Cloud and Chair*) is the work of Spain's most famous living artist, Antoni Tàpies (b.1923). One of the founders of a post-World War II movement christened Dau-al-Set (meaning the die's seventh

ABOVE: *NUVOL I CADIRA (CLOUD AND CHAIR)* SCULPTURE ATOP THE TÀPIES FOUNDATION

face) and descended from Surrealism and Dadaism, Tàpies began as a surrealist but soon became an abstract expressionist, creating a style called 'Arte Povera' in which materials such as string, rags, and waste paper found their way onto his canvases. After 1970 he included larger objects such as pieces of furniture, achieving worldwide fame and influence.
www.fundaciotapies.org

6 Turn right out of Fundació Tàpies and walk up Rambla Catalunya to the far corner with Carrer València for a look at the Bolós Pharmacy and Casa Domènech i Estapá before turning back down this shady promenade.

Art Nouveau and pharmacies hit it off from the start, and rare is the Barcelona pharmacy without Moderniste décor. The Farmacia Bolós is one of the more spectacular, with a stained glass orange tree over the door, a rich mahogany counter, mural and ceiling paintings, and Moderniste glass display cases. The building was designed by architect Josep Domènech i Estapá (1858-1917) in 1902, while the decoration of the pharmacy was the work of Antoni Falguera (1876-1947). For a look at Domènech i Estapá's own house, designed and lived in by the architect, walk across to Carrer Valencia 241. Completed in 1909 as the Moderniste frenzy began to abate, this handsome building, with acid engravings on the entryway glass and curved lines on the façade, reveals the influence of Noucentisme, the more classical movement that followed Art Nouveau.

7 Walk down Rambla de Catalunya all the way to Gran Via de les Corts Catalanes, passing the Casa Garriga Nogués on the corner of Carrer de la Diputació.

The Moderniste Casa Garriga Nogués, at No. 250 Carrer de la Diputació, built in 1904 by Sagnier i Villavecchia, the least Moderniste of the Moderniste architects, is the seat of the Fundación Francisco Godia, which has an excellent collection of paintings starring *Bueyes y barca (Oxen and boat)* by Joaquín Sorolla (1863-1923). Just above Gran Via, look for another Josep Granyer bronze, this one a buffoonish pensive bull called *Meditació*. The Ciudad Condal restaurant is on the left and the Plaça Catalunya metro station is one block down.
www.fundacionfgodia.org

ABOVE: THE FARMACIA BOLÓS

CASA BATLLÓ ROOFTOP

Upper Right Side of the Eixample

This walk takes in a multitude of Moderniste buildings from baronial mansions to the towering temple that has become the city icon.

The right side of the Eixample, La Dreta, where the wealthiest families resided, holds most of the city's Moderniste architecture. Having been excluded from the New World riches that financed the Spanish Golden Age, Catalans had no choice but to develop their own industry, textiles, and by the middle of the 19th century Catalonia was ranked as the 4th most industrialized region in Europe after France, Russia and Germany. This coincided with an artistic and architectural movement known as 'Art Nouveau' in France, 'Modern Style' in England, 'Jugendstil' in Germany, 'Sezessionstil' in Austria, 'Floreale' in Italy, and 'Modernismo' in the rest of Spain. In other parts of Europe, Modernisme was a passing fancy, but in Barcelona this flamboyant style coincided with prosperity and new confidence in Catalan culture and identity as well as with a flair for colour, form and aesthetic exuberance that defines the Catalan temperament, as evidenced by subsequent artists such as Picasso, Miró and Dalí.

From the Diagonal metro station walk east a block to the Palau Baró de Quadras, now home of Casa Àsia.

Palau Baró de Quadras, now occupied by the Casa Àsia business research and cultural centre, is a Puig i Cadafalch building filled with the full range of Moderniste ornamentation. Behind a plateresque (carved with silversmith-like detail) façade built in 1904, the Eusebi Arnau (1846-1918) sculptures are some of his best, especially his inevitable St George slaying the dragon that seems to all but race down the façade. The chalet-like dormer windows across the top floor are a Nordic touch typical of Puig i Cadafalch, who went north for his inspiration, whereas Gaudí and Domènech i Montaner went south, towards Al-Andalus and Mudéjar (Moorish) themes. Asian art is frequently displayed in the upstairs rooms, which have ornate wooden flooring and a stunning horseshoe-shaped fireplace.

CASA ASIA;

www.casaasia.es

2 Cross the Diagonal to the sliver of a block forming a point between Carrer de Còrsega and the Diagonal. On the far side is Casa Comalat, a nearly forgotten Moderniste gem.

At the bottom of Gràcia on Carrer Còrsega at No. 316, this frequently overlooked Moderniste house built in 1911 is one of the city's most interesting Art Nouveau works. Salvador Valeri i Pupurull (1873-1954), who can perhaps

WHERE TO EAT

|O| **OT,**
Carrer de Còrsega 269;
93-488-0977.
Creative contemporary cuisine two blocks from the Sagrada Familia. €€

|❷| **GORRÍA,**
Carrer de la Diputació 421;
93-245-1164.
Traditional Basque cuisine from Navarra in a rustic setting. €€

|❸| **MANAIRÓ,**
Carrer de la Diputació 424;
93-231-0057.
Molecular gastronomy in a sleek contemporary dining room. €€€

be accused of excessive Gaudí influence here, used ballooning multi-coloured ceramic-lined balconies with organic or melting wax-like underpinnings and curious looping wooden galleries. The house is not open to the public.

3 Continue east along the Diagonal to another Puig i Cadafalch Nordic fantasy at the Casa de les Punxes (House of the Spikes).

Casa de les Punxes, also called Casa Terrades for the family for whom it was built, comprises half a dozen conical towers capped with sharp spires. Divided into apartments, space inside is tight and divided vertically into circular triplexes with spiral stairways. Walk around the

101

DISTANCE **2.5 miles (4km)**

ALLOW **3.5 hours**

START **Diagonal metro station**

FINISH **Hospital de Sant Pau metro station**

ABOVE: NATIVITY FAÇADE, SAGRADA FAMÍLIA

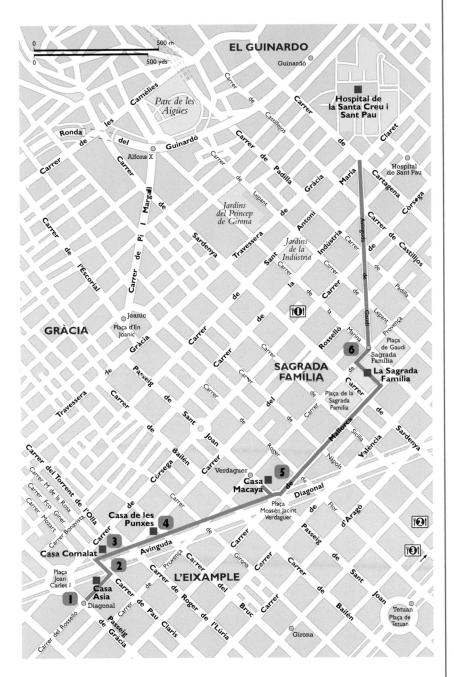

house, one of the very few freestanding Moderniste dwellings. The plaque on the western façade between the conical towers bears an image of St George and reads 'St George, patron saint of Catalunya, return to us our freedom'. Josep Puig i Cadafalch was president of the autonomous Mancomunitat de Catalonia government before the outbreak of the Spanish Civil War; his nationalist Catalan ideas were anathema to the Franco regime, under which he was never allowed to practise his profession after the war ended in 1939.

4 From the Casa de les Punxes continue east on the Diagonal to Passeig de Sant Joan and Casa Macaya, the seat of La Caixa, Spain's cultural mega-foundation.

At Passeig de Sant Joan at No. 108 is the handsome, austere yet playful, Palau Macaya, yet another Puig i Cadafalch creation built in 1901. Sculptor Eusebi Arnau did the figures over the door: a man mounted on a donkey and another on a bicycle, the latter a cameo of Puig i Cadafalch himself who was biking back and forth between Casa Macaya and Casa Amatller on Passeig de Gràcia, with both projects under way at the same time. The white stucco façade is intricately sculpted around the windows, the balcony, and in the asymmetrical entrance hall. A spiky neo-flamboyant Gothic style seemed to be Puig i Cadafalch's eclectic obsession of the moment, having just finished a Nordic castle up the street, a plateresque neo-Renaissance façade at Baró Quadras, and with a Flemish façade in progress at Casa Amatller. The ochre *sgraffito* (see page 32) designs here, by Joan Paradís, are a key part of the ornamentation, as is the wrought iron work by Manuel Ballarin.

5 Turn right on Carrer Mallorca and walk three blocks to Plaça de la Sagrada Familia, the park opposite the Passion façade of Antoni Gaudí's iconic Temple Expiatori de la Sagrada Família (Expiatory Temple of the Holy Family).

Begun in 1882, the Sagrada Família project was taken over the following year by Gaudí, who worked on the structure until his death in 1926. The unfinished church is a symbolic construct with three façades. The lateral façades are the Nativity facade on the east, facing Plaça de Gaudí and the Passion façade on the west, facing Plaça de la Sagrada Família. The Glory façade under construction

ABOVE: SCULPTURE ON THE SAGRADA FAMÍLIA PASSION FAÇADE: *THE ANGUISHED AGNOSTIC*

facing Carrer Mallorca will be the front of the church, and an apartment block between Carrer Mallorca and Carrer València will be demolished to provide an esplanade. The four towers on each façade represent the 12 Apostles. The towers still to be completed include those dedicated to the four evangelists, Matthew, Mark, Luke and John, the Virgin Mary, and the highest of all, dedicated to Christ the Saviour, which will dwarf the other towers and be crowned by an illuminated polychrome ceramic cross at a final height just shorter (because Gaudí felt the work of man should not surpass that of God) than the Montjuïc promontory overlooking the entrance to the port.

www.sagradafamilia.org

6 From the Sagrada Família it's a 20-minute walk to the Hospital Sant Pau, a fully functional Moderniste hospital begun in 1901.

Hospital de Sant Pau is distinguished by its Mudéjar Moorish motifs and lush vegetation. Wards are set in gardens under façades decorated with mosaics. Begun in 1900, the hospital complex won Lluís Domènech i Montaner his third municipal architecture award in 1912. The Moderniste passion for natural and organic forms inspired the architect's conviction that patients would recover better surrounded by trees and flowers than in antiseptic hospital wards. Domènech i Montaner embraced the therapeutic properties of form and colour and filled the hospital with sculptures and mosaics. Originally part of the medieval hospital on Carrer Hospital, the Hospital de Sant Pau moved to this location in 1930. The Hospital Sant Pau metro station is one block from the hospital entrance into Avinguda de Gaudí.

HOSPITAL DE SANT PAU;

www.santpau.es

ABOVE: HOSPITAL DE SANT PAU

INTERIOR OF THE SAGRADA FAMÍLIA

Lower Right Side of the Eixample

This walk delivers a multitude of Moderniste treasures and two of the best Passatges, the intimate alleys that cut through the Eixample blocks.

The lower right side of the Eixample lacks the mega-sites and major attractions of the upper Dreta, such as Gaudí's unfinished colossus. However, the grocery stores, the pharmacies, the market, and the secret passageways and gardens cutting through the chamfered blocks of the great urban grid may come closer to the pulse and true character of life in the middle of this always exciting and passionate Mediterranean metropolis. Contemporary design emporiums such as the Hotel Omm and the BD design store compete with historic Moderniste gems ranging from the Murria grocery store to the Gaudí building that launched his career in the Eixample. With the Mercat de la Concepció open-air produce market at the epicentre of this part of the Eixample, and the many dining options available along the way, from haute cuisine amidst designer architecture to a simple tasting table in a traditional delicatessen, there is no shortage of visual and aromatic excitement along this varied itinerary.

From the Diagonal metro station walk a block down to the corner of Carrer Roselló and turn left for a look in Hotel Omm, before continuing to Carrer de Pau Claris and making a right down to Carrer Mallorca for a left turn to the BD design store at No. 291.

The Hotel Omm is a good place to stop for a coffee or a drink as you pass through the Eixample, a design sanctuary with sleek lines and always entertainingly chic clientele. The various architects and designers at work here sought to create a playful but mystic sense of peace to go with the mantra-like name of the hotel. Upper rooms overlook the roof terrace of Gaudí's Casa Milà. The restaurant, Moo, is the product of the Roca brothers – Joan, Josep and Jordi – famous for their Celler de Can Roca near Girona. A block over to Carrer de Pau Claris and down two and over to Carrer Mallorca No. 291 will reveal the BD (Barcelona Design) store in Casa Thomas, a Moderniste masterpiece by Palau de la Música architect Lluís Domènech i Montaner. A design store in a Moderniste building is a double boon for art and architecture cognoscenti, and if you have extremely deep pockets you can acquire some historic design items here, from the Gaudí Casa Calvet armchair to Dalí's fuchsia Gala love seat. Look for Oscar Tusquets and Javier Mariscal items as well.

2 Walk back to Carrer de Roger de Llúria at the corner of Carrer Mallorca. Feast your eyes on the Moderniste buildings around that corner

before continuing down to Carrer València and the Murria grocery store.

Palau Casades at No. 238 Carrer Mallorca, an eclectic Moderniste structure including classical elements such as the Pompeian patio, is the lawyers' college. Across the street at No. 278 is Palau Montaner, an 1885 building completed by Lluís Domènech i Montaner. Further down on the corner of Carrer València is the Murria store, the most Moderniste grocery store in Barcelona (and the world). The colourful advertisement for Anis del Mono liqueur is taken from a Ramón Casas painting. Across the street at No. 80 Carrer Roger de Llúria is the curious corner tower of the Casa Villanueva, built in 1906 by Juli M. Fossas i Martinez, a relatively unknown Moderniste apparently influenced by Domènech i Montaner's Casa Lleó Morera.

DISTANCE 2.5 miles (4km)

ALLOW 3.5 hours

START Diagonal metro station

FINISH Plaça Catalunya metro station

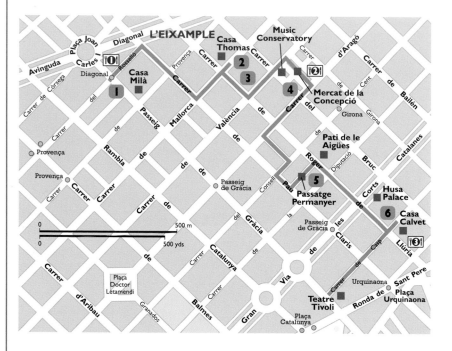

3 Walk east on Carrer València across Carrer del Bruc, past the Music Conservatory and down through the Mercat de la Concepció to Carrer d'Aragó.

A walk to the east takes you past the Music Conservatory, a Noucentiste work by architect Antoni Falguera (who designed the Bolós pharmacy in Walk 13), on the corner of Carrer del Bruc. This imposing, stolid structure displays Noucentiste's characteristic weightiness,

as if embarrassed by Moderniste's ornamental madness. Next on the right is the Mercat de la Concepció, a glass and steel structure always bursting at the seams with delightful flowers and food, and at the far side, Passatge del Mercat and Passatge del Pla, with the excellent restaurant Pep at the edge of the market. Just down on Carrer d'Aragó to the right is Mantemeria Can Ravell, where one can taste everything from the top anchovies to the best *jamón ibérico de bellota* (acorn-fed wild Ibérico ham).

OPPOSITE: CASA VILLANUEVA

WHERE TO EAT

|O| MOO,
Carrer Roselló 265;
93-445-4000.
Postmodern gastronomy from the
Roca brothers in the designer
Hotel Omm. €€€

|O| MANTEQUERIA CAN RAVELL,
Carrer d'Aragó 313;
93-457-5114.
Restaurant and tasters' nirvana with
the finest of everything. €€

|O| CASA CALVET,
Carrer Casp 48;
93-412-4012.
Elegant Mediterranean and Catalan
fare in a Gaudí building. €€€

4 Walk to the right down Carrer
d'Aragó, cross at the corner of
Carrer de Roger de Llúria and take the
Passatge de Méndez Vigo through the
block to Carrer del Consell de Cent.
Another right, left and left turn will
traverse Passatge Permanyer to the
Jardins de la Torre de les Aïgues.

Carrer d'Aragó is a six-lane motorway
not to be trifled with or, for that matter,
frequented: a place for noisy, fast and
greedy drivers obsessed with crossing
Barcelona at the speed of light. Cross
to the lower side of Carrer d'Aragó
and look for the verdant Passatge de
Méndez Vigo that cuts through the
block to Carrer Consell de Cent. A
wide wrought-iron archway leads down
between the Italian School and the Italian
Cultural Centre, both hidden away in
this overgrown oasis surrounded by some
of the city's most urban thoroughfares.
The far end of the passage is occasionally
closed, meaning a loop back around,
but normally it's open and a quick
right to Carrer de Pau Claris and a
left down to Passatge Permanyer leads
through an even more surprising garden
community, a series of tiny houses and
gardens modelled on London's Regent's
Park terraces of formal town houses.
Artists, poets and musicians have always
loved Passatge Permanyer, and Apel.les
Mestres (1854-1936), who was all three –
illustrator, poet and composer – was the
most famous of them all. At the far end
of Passatge Permanyer, a tunnel at No. 56
Roger de Llúria leads into the charming
Pati de les Aigües, where a children's
swimming pool and palm trees fill a
hidden space tucked in behind the rear
of Eixample apartment buildings.

5 Walk down Carrer Roger de Llúria
across Gran Via de les Corts
Catalanes to the ex-Hotel Ritz (now the
Hotel Palace). Continue down another
block and turn left on Carrer de Casp
to Casa Calvet.

Two blocks down from the Pati de les
Aigües is the Gran Via de les Corts
Catalanes, with the Venancio Valmitjana
(1830-1919) sculpture of Diana, Roman
goddess of the hunt, the moon, and
protector of the forest and of wildlife
splashing in the middle of the divided

boulevard. The legendary Hotel Ritz, now called the Hotel Palace, stands at the far side of the intersection at No. 668, a good place for a drink in the rambling tea rooms or at the cool dark, wood and leather-lined downstairs bar. Another block down and half a block to the left is Gaudí's first Eixample house, Casa Calvet, built in 1900 for the textile baron Pere Calvet. Symbols on the facade range from the owner's stylized 'C' over the door to the cypress, symbol of hospitality. The wild mushrooms on the main floor reflect Calvet's (and Gaudí's) passion for fungi, while the busts at the top are St Peter, the owner's patron saint; St Genis of Arles and St Genis of Rome, patrons of Vilassar, the Calvet family's home town north of Barcelona. For more Gaudí (or at least Gaudí-esque décor), dine next door at the excellent Casa Calvet restaurant.

6 Walk back toward Passeig de Gràcia on Carrer Casp to the Teatre Tivoli and, just a block left, Plaça de Catalunya.

The walk back along Carrer Casp passes several buildings of note, the Casa de Sant Jordi at the corner of Carrer de Pau Claris and at No. 22 the Casa Camprubí. The Tivoli Theatre is a famous Barcelona landmark, a dance, theatre and cinema venue for more than a century. The Café Bracafé (Brasil Café) just in from Passeig de Gràcia is always alluring, whether in the rain, in the dead of winter, or when the pavement terrace is filled to capacity in summer; the quintessential cosmopolitan hideaway for a cup of coffee and a hurried breakfast.

From Bracafé, the Plaça Catalunya metro is just out to Passeig de Gràcia and to the left a block.

113

Left Side of the Eixample

The left side of the grid square labyrinth of the Eixample has fewer Moderniste houses, but those it has are among the most extraordinary.

The left side of the Eixample, L'Esquerra, traditionally considered the working class side of the post-1860 expansion that allowed the city to finally move beyond its medieval ramparts, is less densely packed with Moderniste architecture than the right side. Around Plaça d'Espanya and along Gran Via de les Corts Catalanes is a miscellany of monuments, townhouses, gardens and squares in a bustling urban area filled with restaurants, bars and boutiques. Beginning at Plaça Espanya, built for the 1929 International Exposition, and exploring the Parc de Joan Miró and surrounding streets, this walk proceeds into the centre of the city along the Gran Via de les Corts Catalanes, with occasional detours into the semi-secret gardens of the Eixample's city blocks. Casa de la Papallona (the House of the Butterfly) and Casa Golferichs are two of the least visited and most spectacular of the city's many Moderniste houses, while the Central University's Patio de les Lletres remains well off the beaten path.

From Plaça d'Espanya take a look at the central fountain and the Venetian towers before walking up Carrer de Tarragona to the Parc de Joan Miró.

Plaça d'Espanya is a carousel of automobiles and buses spinning traffic off into no fewer than six major arteries headed to the airport, city centre, the convention grounds, the Sants neighbourhood, the train station, and via the Paral.lel, the port. The Venetian Towers on the south side of the square were erected for the 1929 International Exposition, as was the square itself, until then a slum densely populated with gypsies and the poorest immigrants from all over Spain living in a shantytown. The fountain in the centre of Plaça d'Espanya was designed by Gaudí collaborator Josep Maria Jujol (1879-1949, creator of the famous serpentine Park Güell benches), while the sculptural work was done by Moderniste sculptor Miquel Blay (1866-1936), creator of the Palau de la Música Catalana's homage to Catalan popular song. The Les Arenas (The Sands) bullring, currently being turned into an entertainment and commercial complex with cinemas, restaurants and a rock & roll museum, was once an important bullfighting venue, but the Moderniste Monumental bullring across town is now the city's sole tauromachy option. The neo-Mudéjar (exposed brick and horsehoe arches) bullring façade was built in 1898 and has been abandoned since 1990. Parc de Joan Miró, also known as Parc de l'Escorxador (Abattoir), as the slaughterhouse for the bullring was

115

DISTANCE **2 miles (3.2km)**

ALLOW **2.5 hours**

START **Plaça d'Espanya metro station**

FINISH **Universitat metro station**

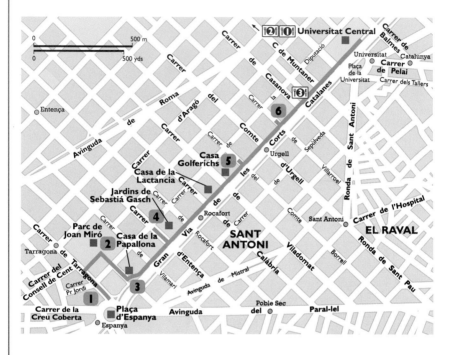

located there, is dominated by the Joan Miró sculpture entitled *Dona i Ocell (Woman and Bird)*, a clear clue to Miró's Freud-influenced surrealist beginnings.

2 From Parc de Joan Miró, walk out the northeast corner of the square across Carrer de la Diputació into Carrer Llança and down to the Casa de la Papallona at No. 9.

Casa Fajol, known as the Casa de la Papallona for the yellow and green

butterfly (*papallona*) made of mosaic ceramic tiles broken into pieces, a popular Moderniste technique for lining curved surfaces, was built in 1912 by Josep Graner i Prat. The building, curiously, remains innocent of Moderniste intent until the top of the façade.

For a better look at the butterfly, possibly the most outrageous and whimsical effect in all of Barcelona's Moderniste architecture, retreat back across the street to the island in the middle of Gran Via.

3 Begin the long, noisy but interesting walk northeast along Gran Via de les Corts Catalanes, looking for the Casa de la Lactancia at No. 475-477.

Two blocks down Gran Via, a detour to the left up Carrer d'Entença leads up the right side of the street to the Jardins de Sebastiá Gasch at No. 88. These interior gardens were nearly all filled with construction by owners, though some remain. Back on the Gran Via, the Casa de la Lactancia (Nursing Mothers' House) at No. 475–477 is a lovely bluish colour with floral motifs and an Eusebi Arnau sculpture on the theme of breastfeeding over the entryway. Completed in 1913 by Antoni Falguera and Pere Falqués, the interior courtyard with an ample skylight is the architectural highlight.

4 Continue ahead on Gran Via to Casa Golferichs at No. 491.

Casa Golferichs, known as 'El Xalet' (the chalet), evoking a Swiss chalet in the Bern mountains around Gstaad, is composed of ample woodwork as well as stone and ceramics, with sloping eaves and an intimate, cozy feel. The art gallery inside is open to the public as is the upstairs concert and lecture hall when musical events are scheduled. Built in 1901 by Moderniste architect Joan Rubió i Bellver for Macaro Golferichs, an importer of tropical woods, Casa

Golferichs was in danger of demolition in the late 1960s when its owner planned to build an apartment block with underground parking, but public outcry and social pressure halted the project.

5 Walk east on the Gran Via, looking for Carrer del Comte Borrell for a detour left to the Madroñal pharmacy and, further along, Carrer de Vilarroel, where the Mestre pharmacy offers another example of Modernisme.

At Carrer del Comte Borrell, a three-minute walk up to the left, the Farmacia Madroñal at No. 133 is a Moderniste colony. Two blocks further on the corner of Gran Via and Vilarroel, the Farmacia Mestre still has the original doors and windows. A short walk up to the left on Vilarroel leads to another hidden garden at No. 70, Jardins de Cèsar Martinell. At the same corner, at No. 536–542, are three Moderniste apartment buildings.

6 Continue ahead on Gran Via de les Corts Catalanes to the immense Universitat de Barcelona building at Plaça de la Universitat.

From the north pavement of Gran Via, look across to the building at No. 582, a block before the university. Casa Gerónimo Granell was built by the architect for himself in 1902. His unusual use of Neo-Gothic elements gives this Moderniste house, which has undergone a series of renovations and reforms, a distinctive flavour. Across Carrer Aribau on the left is the central university.

WHERE TO EAT

🍽 CINC SENTITS,
Carrer Aribau 93;
93-323-9490.
A Catalan-Canadian family creating avant-garde contemporary cuisine. €€€

🍽 TAKTIKA BERRI,
Carrer València 169;
93-453-4759.
Basque cooking from San Sebastián and peerless tapas. €€

🍽 MEXITERRANÉE,
Gran Via de les Corts Catalanes 559;
93-285-3834.
Mediterranean-Mexican fusion cuisine in contemporary boutique hotel. €€€

Barcelona has university buildings scattered all over town, but this is the oldest part of the complex left standing in the city centre. Built by Elies Rogent between 1861 and 1889, it has a series of gardens and courtyards. The Pati de les Lletres (Patio of Letters) just inside the left entryway is the most graceful space in the complex, with orange and cypress trees around a pretty courtyard. Through the side exit to the left is a lush garden that leads around the back of the building past pools and fountains to the grand stairway up to the Paraninfo auditorium and back to the street. The Universitat metro stop is directly across the square, while the Plaça Catalunya stop is just a five-minute walk through Carrer de Pelai.

Gaudí's Park Güell

Park Güell is one of the city's magical spots, where Gaudí unleashes a playful, humorous side that some of his darker creations partially conceal.

Gaudí and his patron Count Eusebi Güell (1846-1918) developed Park Güell between 1900 and 1914. Güell thought the project would attract Barcelona's wealthiest families to leave the city hubbub in favour of the peace and quiet of a secluded garden community in the hills. Luckily for Park Güell's many visitors over the last century, the Barcelona bourgeoisie showed little interest in moving further away from the social and cultural resources of downtown Barcelona, a tendency that persists, at least partially, to this day. Inspired by the British Mayfair Garden suburbs (the English spelling for the word Park is original and deliberate), 60 plots were to be sold for single family homes. Only two houses were standing when in 1923 the municipal authorities were given the park by the Güell family. Everything in it is singular: the gingerbread gatehouses, the psychedelic lizard, the market with 86 leaning columns, the slanted corridor under leaning tree trunks, the undulating bench, and the Gaudí house, now a museum.

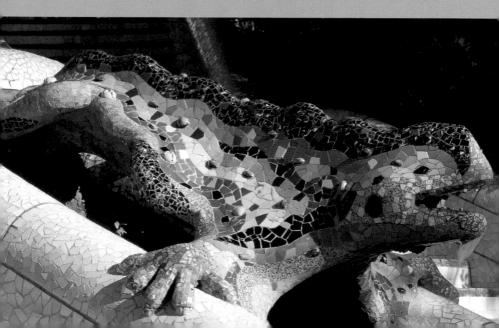

I From Plaça de Lesseps walk west along the bottom of the square before cutting into Carrer de Santa Perpètua in upper Gràcia. Turn up to Travessera de Dalt on Carrer Verdi and walk right for five minutes to the corner of Carrer de Larrard. Turn left and walk a steep 15 minutes to the entrance to Park Güell on Carrer d'Olot.

Plaça de Lesseps is named for Ferdinand de Lesseps, engineer of the Suez and Panama canals, a Barcelona hero from the year 1842, when, as Consul-General of France, he saved many people during a violent uprising, ending with the bombardment of the city by Madrid forces. Carrer Larrard is punctuated with one-family *torres* (towers), as small separate houses are called in Barcelona. The entryway into Park Güell has two small gatehouses on either side, topped with 'wild mushrooms', on the right the red, white-specked fly ammanite of *Alice in Wonderland* fame, and on the left, the *Phallus impudicus*, a remarkably priapic mushroom that sprouts and disappears within a few hours. Gaudí's standard Greek cross also towers over the left gatehouse. The bookstore in the left gatehouse is filled with Moderniste and Gaudí literature, while the right gatehouse is the Centre d'Interpretació del Park Güell, with videos and displays explaining the features of the park.

2 Walk directly ahead up the staircase by the kaleidoscopic lizard and into the forest of leaning columns at the top of the steps.

WHERE TO EAT

󰀀 CAN CORTADA,
Avinguda Estatut de Catalunya 88;
93-427-2315.
A gorgeous 16th-century country manor serving Catalan cuisine. €€€

󰀀 BODEGA MANOLO,
Torrent de les Flors 101;
93-284-4377.
A tiny back room dining space serving fine fare in upper Gràcia. €€

󰀀 RINCÓN DEL CAZADOR,
Pg. Mare de Déu del Coll 68;
93-213-3860.
Game dishes and meats cooked over coals above Park Güell. €€

The famous Gaudí lizard, like much of the most playful work in Park Güell, was done in collaboration with Josep Maria Jujol (1879-1949), a fellow Moderniste architect. This lizard or dragon is another reference to the St George and dragon legend that appears throughout Barcelona's Moderniste statuary. Behind the dragon-lizard is the *quatre barres*, the four bars of the Catalan flag. At the top of the steps, 86 leaning Doric columns support the esplanade above. This area was designed as a covered produce market for the 60 families of the original garden community, and now provides shelter and acoustics for the musicians who play here.

3 Walk to the left and climb the stairway up to the beginning of the

DISTANCE **2 miles (3.2km)**

ALLOW **3 hours**

START **Plaça de Lesseps metro station**

FINISH **Plaça de Lesseps metro station**

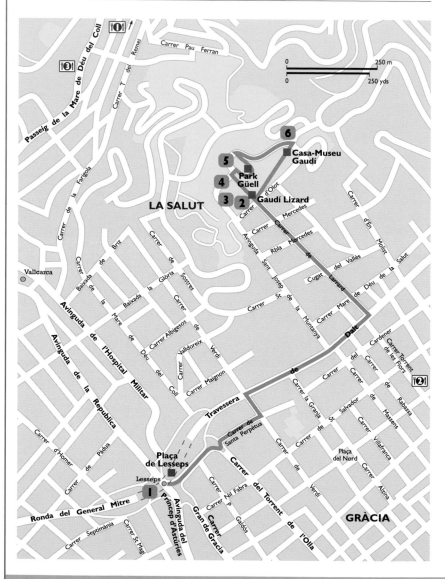

OPPOSITE: PARK GÜELL 'HYPOSTYLE' MARKET

ABOVE: GAUDÍ'S GATEHOUSES WITH RED AND WHITE SPECKLED FLY AMMANITE ON THE LEFT

covered corridor that can be seen curving out to the left.

The so-called *bugadera* (washerwoman) covered corridor is lined with leaning tree-like columns made of stone and earth from the park. The effect is a trompe l'oeil slant under a tear-shaped overhead arch. On a column at the end of the corridor is the washerwoman herself with a large vat of laundry on her head.

4 Walk back to the start of the corridor and up to the wide esplanade with the undulating ceramic bench curving around the Mediterranean side of the square.

The serpentine bench ringing this open space is one of Gaudí's most iconic elements even though it is well known that the young Josep Maria Jujol was the architect who put it together. Using the technique of *trencadis*, or broken bits of tile (*trencar* means 'to break' in Catalan), Jujol designed an undulating bench that is particularly spectacular, as is all of Park Güell, when the sun is high or waning and its colours and the city below (and the Mediterranean beyond) are illuminated from the west.

5 Walk around the esplanade to the cafés and ice cream stand at its base and turn right towards the Casa-Museu Gaudí visible north of the Jujol Bench.

The salmon-coloured chalet a few steps to the right is the house where Gaudí lived for 20 years with his niece.

Built by Francesc Berenguer i Mestres (1866-1914), his right-hand man and foreman, this little chalet is filled with Gaudí memorabilia and photographs. Never successful in his love life (his tendency to obsession apparently scared love objects away), Gaudí himself affirmed that he had 'no vocation for married life'. No one, especially the Catholic right that is working hard to have Gaudí canonized, has ever suggested that Gaudí's relationship with his niece was anything more than an alliance of convenience. Berenguer i Mestres, on the other hand, was pressed into Gaudí's service in part through his own marital successes (seven children). Berenguer, needing to support his rapidly growing family, dropped out of architecture school and signed on with Gaudí while in his 20s, becoming indispensable to Gaudí's productivity. After Berenguer's death in 1914, Gaudí worked only on his Sagrada Família project, making little progress.

6 Walk down and to the right from Casa-Museu Gaudí and continue through the usually flower-bedecked gardens back to the entrance.

The lush lower part of Park Güell is the prettiest, with lovers spread out in the grass and picnics commonplace. A walk down into upper Gràcia along Carrer Torrent de les Flors will lead to Bodega Manolo and other Gràcia restaurants, whereas a taxi a little further north will reach Can Cortada in under 10 minutes. The Plaça de Lesseps metro station is a 20-minute walk downhill.

JUJOL'S SERPENTINE MOSAIC BENCH IN PARK GÜELL

Radical Chic in Gràcia

Gràcia is a universe within a city (Barcelona) within a nation (Catalonia) within a state (Spain). Most of all it is a rogue district loved by the young.

Gràcia, an outlying village, has always had an independent spirit. Workers here began resisting industrialization almost before textile barons invented factories. An uprising in 1856 turned bloody when the soldiers sent to quell the disturbance were lynched and double the number of Gràcia revolutionaries were executed in reprisal. Later, in 1870, a furious brigade of Gràcia mothers burned the town archives and barricaded the streets to protest against military conscription of young *graciencs* to fight Spain's colonial battles in North Africa, leading to an army artillery barrage on the village. Even the names of the streets – Llibertat, Fraternitat, Progrès, Revolució – suggest Gràcia's commitment to radical causes such as justice and solidarity, so it's no wonder that young people feel at home here. Bars, cinemas, shops and restaurants proliferate along Gràcia's intimate alleys and streets, while terrace cafés and taverns in Plaça del Sol and Plaça Rius i Taulet turn into all-night street parties on warm evenings.

From the Fontana metro station, walk across Carrer Gran de Gràcia to Carrer Bretón de Los Herreros and over to the corner of Carrer de les Carolines. Go right one block to Casa Vicens, Gaudí's first major work.

Commissioned in 1883 by a ceramics merchant eager to advertise his wares, Barcelona's first polychromatic tile house marked Gaudí's debut as an architect. Still dependent on the traditional tools of architecture, in this case the T-square, Casa Vicens shows none of the organic shapes and looping arches of classic Gaudí. Mudéjar motifs make the façade a striking geometrical chequerboard. The chemaro palm leaves decorating the gate and fence are the work of Gaudí's right-hand man, Francesc Berenguer, though the jokey lizards and bats in the wrought iron are Gaudí's playful send-up of the Gothic gargoyle. Closed to the public, the interior is even more spectacular than the façade, with trompe l'oeil birds painted on the salon walls and an intricately carved ceiling in the smoking room that could be part of the Alhambra.

2 Walk across Carrer de les Carolines to Gran de Gràcia and go right down to Plaça Trilla. Walk through Plaça Trilla, go right on Carrer de Trilla to Carrer de Santa Rosa. Turn left to Carrer de Badia, right to Carrer d'Àstúries, and then left into Plaça del Diamant.

Plaça del Diamant, named for a precious stone as are many of Gràcia's streets

(Robi, Or, Perla, Topazi) thanks to a 19th-century jeweller-mayor, is a sought-after Gràcia address as a result of the novel of the same name by Mercé Rodoreda, Catalonia's finest novelist until the winners of the Spanish Civil War outlawed her language in 1939. The bronze sculpture to the right as you enter the square depicts the novel's protagonist, Colometa, uttering her famous scream, Rodoreda's literary version of the Munch painting: '…a scream I must have been carrying around inside me for many years, so thick it was hard for it to get through my throat, and with that scream,

OPPOSITE: 'RUTH' BRONZE AND TERRACE CAFÉ IN PLAÇA DE LA VIRREINA; ABOVE: CASA VICENS

DISTANCE 1.5 miles (2.4km)

ALLOW 3 hours

START Fontana metro station

FINISH Diagonal metro station

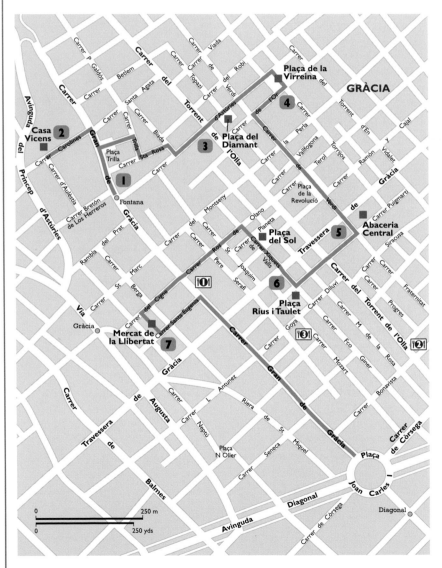

a little bit of nothing trickled out of my mouth, like a cockroach made of spit… and that bit of nothing that had lived so long trapped inside me was my youth, and it flew off with a scream of I don't know what…letting go?'.

3 From Plaça del Diamant, continue across Carrer de Verdi on Carrer d'Astúries to Plaça de la Virreina.

Plaça de la Virreina is named for the young widow of the Viceroy of Perú, Maria Francesca Fivaller, a descendant of the famous 13th-century city mayor Joan Fivaller. The bronze figure in the square is a sculpture of Ruth, the Old Testament's paradigmatic faithful wife, who served her husband Boaz's family after his death, just as Maria Francesca Fivaller remained faithful to the Viceroy, using his fortune to perform good works for the city. The church of Sant Joan (St John), many times destroyed and restored, overlooks the square. At Carrer d'Or No. 44 is a building by Francesc Berenguer, Gaudí's assistant, who built a dozen important Gràcia buildings, even though he was officially unable to sign his work, never having finished his degree. Berenguer's vast importance in Gaudí's work has been the subject of much research and speculation. This building is one of his best, a steep, vertical apartment with ornate wrought-iron balconies and *sgraffito* (see page 32) designs.

4 From the downhill edge of Plaça de la Virreina, walk one block to the right and turn left down Carrer de Verdi.

WHERE TO EAT

|O| BOTAFUMEIRO,
Carrer Gran de Gràcia 81;
93-218-4230.
The best place to enjoy Galician seafood and Albariño white wines in the centre of Gràcia. €€€

|O| BILBAO,
Carrer Perill 33;
93-458-9624.
Excellent Catalan cuisine in a relaxed and easygoing setting. €€

|O| IPAR-TXOKO,
Carrer Mozart 22;
93-218-1954.
Basque cooking at its best, gracefully served in a small and attractive dining room. €€

Carrer Verdi is a well-known cinema street, with the Verdi theatre at No. 32, and the Verdi Park around the block at Carrer Torrijos 49. Both are famous for films shown in their original languages. Carrer Verdi also has numerous cozy restaurants busy with post- and pre-movie-goers. Amrit at No. 18 serves excellent Libyan food. Plaça de la Revolució opens up at the bottom of Carrer Verdi.

Through Mare de Déu dels Desamparats at the bottom of the square is the Mercat de la Revolució, now officially entitled Abaceria Central, another colourful display of food produce and a good place to pause.

5 Walk from the market to the right on Carrer de Puigmartí to Plaça Rius i Taulet, the central square of the village of Gràcia.

Plaça Rius i Taulet, named after a 19th-century Barcelona mayor, is popularly known as the Plaça del Rellotge, clocktower square, for the handsome brick clock and bell tower standing at its centre. This is the tower bombarded by Spanish artillery in 1870. The severely damaged bell was not repaired for years as a memorial to lives lost. The handsome royal blue building at the lower end of the square is the Gràcia town hall, by Francesc Berenguer.

6 From Plaça Rius i Taulet, walk up to Plaça del Sol on Carrer Mariana Pineda and Carrer Xiquets de Valls. Continue walking up to Carrer Ros de Olano, turn left, and then walk out across Carrer Gran de Gràcia to the Carrer del Cigne and the Mercat de la Llibertat.

Plaça del Sol is Gràcia's second square after Plaça Rius i Taulet, well populated with cafés, nightspots and terrace hangouts popular with college students and young partiers. Carrer Ros de Olano leads left out to Carrer Gran de Gràcia past another Francesc Berenguer building at No. 9, the Centre Moral Instructiu de Gràcia, a social and cultural club of which Berenguer was President. The Mercat de la Llibertat is another lovely steel hangar semi-open air market designed, again, by Francesc Berenguer.

7 Walk though the market, emerging into Carrer Santa Eugenia. Return to Carrer Gran de Gràcia. Turn right and walk all the way down to the Diagonal.

Carrer Gran de Gràcia has a trove of Moderniste buildings lining the right side of the street headed downhill towards the sea. Many of these houses were designed by Francesc Berenguer, though signed by other architects. Nos. 61, 51, 35, 23 and 15 are all Berenguer suspects, gorgeous Moderniste buildings with stained-glass galleries and scrolled, floral relief over the windows and balconies. At the bottom of Gran de Gràcia, Casa Fuster, a late Domènech i Montaner building erected between 1908 and 1911, is one of only two Barcelona hotels housed in Moderniste buildings. Passeig de Gràcia and the Diagonal metro station are just through the Jardins de Salvador Espriu and across the Diagonal.

OPPOSITE: PLAÇA DEL SOL; ABOVE: CASA FUSTER

Montjuïc: Catalonia's Art Treasury

The Museu Nacional d'Art de Catalunya, the Joan Miró foundation and Caixafòrum's temporary exhibits provide enough art to last a lifetime.

Art lovers can easily spend a full day on Montjuïc, if not a full week. The promontory overlooking the south side of the Barcelona harbour port is thought to have originally been named Mont Juif for a medieval Jewish cemetery, though a Roman document citing a road between Mons Taber (around the cathedral) and Mons Jovis (Mount of Jove) would indicate that Montjuïc may derive from the Roman deity Jove, or Jupiter. Walking Montjuïc is a serious march compared to street life-rich promenades in the rest of Barcelona, and looking at paintings is already a challenge, so be prepared to grab a cab if the need arises. The Miró Foundation, the Romanesque collection of Pyrenean frescoes in the Palau Nacional (MNAC), the minimalist Mies van der Rohe Pavilion, and the gallery and auditorium Caixafòrum (Casaramona) are among Barcelona's must-see sights. The Castell de Montjuïc fortress, the Olympic Stadium and the Palau Sant Jordi are worth a brief look.

From the Paral.lel metro station, catch the Montjuïc funicular up to the Av. Miramar station. Walk right, away from the Mediterranean, for 15 minutes to the Joan Miró Foundation.

Joan Miró's gift to his native city is one of Barcelona's finest contemporary art venues. The glass and steel building with views north over Barcelona was designed by Josep Lluis Sert and opened in 1975 Miró's childlike, colourful style, bright with Mediterranean light and whimsy, is a perfect match for its architectural environment. Alexander Calder's fountain of moving mercury is one of the stars of the Miró Foundation. During the Franco regime, which he opposed, Miró lived in self-imposed exile in Paris before moving to Majorca in 1956. When he died in 1983, Catalonia devoted a massive send-off to an artist who captured the artistic idiosyncrasy of his fellow Catalans. Miró's shooting blue star is the logo of La Caixa, Barcelona's gigantic cultural foundation, and is an iconic brand nearly as familiar and recognizable as the red and yellow-striped Catalan *senyera* (flag).

2 From the Miró Foundation walk 20 minutes along Avinguda de l'Estadi to the Olympic stadium and the Palau Sant Jordi, or cut straight through the Jardins de Laribal to the Museu Nacional d'Art de Catalunya.

This is the best moment to view the Olympic Stadium, built for the 1936 Olympic Games subsequently held in Berlin and renovated for Barcelona's

WHERE TO EAT

[O] **OLEUM,**
Palau Nacional (MNAC);
93-289-0679.
Creative Mediterranean cooking in a stupendous venue with stunning views. €€€

[O] **FUNDACIÓ JOAN MIRÓ,**
Av. Miramar 1;
93-329-0768.
Light Mediterranean cuisine in a Sert building surrounded by Miró paintings. €€

[O] **RIAS DE GALICIA,**
Carrer Lleida 7;
93-424-8152.
Galician seafood just a step from the Magic Fountain below the MNAC. €€€

1992 Olympics. The Palau Sant Jordi, the gigantic Arata Isozaki sports and concert venue is nearby, with the Santiago Calatrava communications tower overhead. The Museu Nacional d'Art de Catalunya (MNAC), built as the main pavilion for Barcelona's 1929 International Exhibition, was never meant to last forever. Regarded through much of the 20th century as an enormous eyesore, the building began to fall apart in the late 1970s, to the relief of many. In the end, the Palau Nacional was saved and restored and now contains the full measure of 1000 years of Catalan art, from Romanesque to the present. The

135

DISTANCE **3.5 miles (2.4km)**

ALLOW **6 hours**

START **Funicular de Montjuïc (Paral.lel metro station)**

FINISH **Plaça d'Espanya metro station**

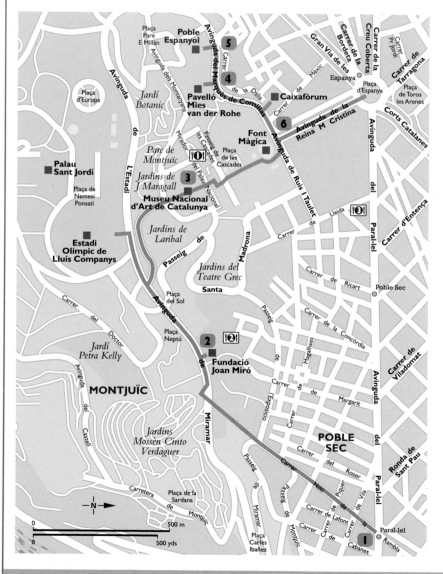

OPPOSITE: THE SANTIAGO CALATRAVA 'PURULI' OVER THE ARATA ISOZAKI PALAU SANT JORDI

original collections: Romanesque, Gothic, Renaissance and Baroque, and the Cambó Collection (donated by financier Francesc Cambó) were joined by the Thyssen-Bornemisza and Art Modern collections in 2004. The Romanesque murals were removed from chapels in the Pyrenees during the 1920s to preserve them from deterioration and theft. Reproductions of the finest friezes have been restored to their original settings in remote Pyrenean valleys.

The Gothic collection contains treasures from Catalonia's Gothic golden age including works by Jaume Huguet, and Bernat Martorell. The Renaissance and Baroque collection includes work by Ribera, Tiépolo, El Greco, and Zurbarán. The Thyssen-Bornemisza collection covers the period between the Gothic and Rococo with paintings by Rubens, Zurbarán, Tintoretto, and Velázquez. The Art Modern star is Marià Fortuny (1838-74), whose stunning battlefield painting *La Batalla de Tetuán* covers an entire wall of room No. 62. The Olot school of landscape painters, the Moderniste painters Rusiñol and Casas, the Catalan impressionist Nonell, and a potpourri of painters including Boudin, Sisley, Romero de Torres, Regoyos, Sorolla, Zuloaga, and Gutiérrez Solana complete this staggering concentration of 19th- and early 20th-century artists. Oleum restaurant makes an excellent lunch stop, and, in winter, the Magic Fountain's music and light show will be starting up at around the same time that the MNAC closes.

MNAC; www.mnac.es

3 From the MNAC, walk down the main stairs up from Plaça d'Espanya to the Magic Fountain and turn left to the Mies van der Rohe Pavilion.

The Magic Fountain performs a music and light show every evening at sundown, so the time varies during the year. The Mies van der Rohe Barcelona Pavilion was built for the 1929 Universal Exhibition and reassembled between 1983 and 1986. The interlocking planes of white marble, green onyx, and glass is the city's aesthetic bookend for the Art Nouveau Palau de la Música. Highlights: the matching grain of the green onyx panels, black carpet mirror of the reflecting pool with the graceful bronze nude, the Barcelona chair designed by Ludwig Mies van der Rohe (1886-1969). The Mies van der Rohe store sells interesting design-related knick-knacks ranging from 'Less is more' T-shirts to kits for building your own mini-pavilion at home.

AV. MARQUÈS DE COMILLAS S/N;
TEL: 93/423—4016
www.miesbcn.com

4 Walk up Av. del Marquès de Comillas to Poble Espanyol, an often underrated anthology of Spain's most beautiful architecture.

Another 1929 International Exhibition production, Poble Espanyol (Spanish Village) takes you from walled Castilian towns to Andalusian villages. For a full survey of Spain's architecture, with quality artisans and craftsmen making

everything from leathers to silk scarves and mantillas along the way, Poble Espanyol is a fascinating visit to a lovingly recreated ersatz Spain. The Fundació Fran Daurel displays temporary exhibits, while a reservation at the Tablao del Carmen flamenco club, one of the best in Barcelona, includes free access to the rest of the complex.

5 Walk back down Avinguda Marquès de Comillas to Caixafòrum, an art gallery and cultural centre in a restored old textile factory.

This redbrick, neo-Mudéjar Art Nouveau fortress, built to house a factory in 1911 by Josep Puig i Cadafalch, is a centre for art exhibits, concerts, lectures and cultural events. Well worth following in daily listings, Casaramona, now Caixafòrum, has been given a second life as one of Barcelona's leading art venues.

The restoration is another example of Barcelona's talent for combining modern design techniques with traditional architecture. The Arata Isozaki–designed foyer and entryway, as well as the Caixafòrum store, have won design prizes. www.fundacio.lacaixa.es

6 Walk down to Plaça d'Espanya through Avinguda de la Reina Maria Cristina and the Fira de Barcelona, the city convention grounds.

The walk down Avinguda de la Reina Maria Cristina offers panoramas of the Palau Nacional and the Magic Fountain behind and the Venetian Towers ahead at the edge of Plaça d'Espanya. The Rias de Galicia restaurant is to the right out Av. Rius i Taulet on Carrer de Lleida, serving nonstop from 1pm to 1am. The Plaça d'Espanya metro station connects with Plaça de Catalunya in under 10 minutes.

139

'MAGIC FOUNTAIN' WITH THE TOPS OF THE VENETIAN TOWERS OVER PLAÇA D'ESPANYA IN BACKGROUND

Park, Zoo and Parliament at La Ciutadella

This citadel turned park offers leafy promenades, proto-Gaudí rocks, the city's first Moderniste architecture, museums, sculpture and the zoo.

Barcelona's city-centre park, La Ciutadella, was originally a fortress built by the conquering army of the Bourbon King Felipe V after the fall of Barcelona in the 1700-14 War of the Spanish Succession. It was the fortress and its outbuildings that required over 1000 houses in the Barrio de la Ribera to be dismantled to create fields of fire for the La Ciutadella artillery guarding the rebellious Catalans. The Ciutadella fortress, a hated symbol of foreign oppression, where Catalan patriots were imprisoned and executed, was finally decommissioned as a military fortress in 1869, when the Spanish dictator General Prim ceded it to the city on the condition that it be made into a public park. Josep Fontseré i Mestres designed the park in 1872 and it opened to the public in 1877. The Universal Exhibition of 1888 gave the park Barcelona's first Moderniste building, now the Museum of Zoology, while the Catalan Parliament and the city zoo complete the Ciutadella's diverse attractions.

From the Arc de Triomf metro stop, walk underneath the triumphal arch and start walking down Passeig de Lluís Companys.

This massive redbrick triumphal arch built by Josep Vilaseca in 1888 commemorates the 1229 conquest of Mallorca, as suggested by the bats portrayed overhead. Bats were, curiously, the imperial symbol of Jaume I el Conqueridor (James I the Conqueror) (1208-76), allegedly because bats had helped him in battle by waking his troops in time to repel a Moorish attack. Other sculptures on the arch depict visitors to the Universal Exhibition arriving and receiving prizes.

2 Continue down Passeig Lluís de Companys to the entrance into the Parc de la Ciutadella.

On the way down this wide promenade, the grandiose building to the left is the Palau de Justicia (Palace of Justice). To the right are other courthouses and legal facilities Lluís Companys, the last President of the Generalitat at the end of the Spanish Civil War, for whom the promenade is named, would no doubt have wished to be put on trial in these civil courtrooms when he was handed over by the Gestapo to Franco forces in 1940 after being arrested in Paris. The military court martial promptly (and ironically) convicted Companys of 'military rebellion' and executed him by firing squad in the moat of the Castell de Montjuïc on 15 October 1940.

3 Entering the park, turn right to the Museu de Ciències Naturals and the Edificio de Zoologia, known as the Castell dels Tres Dragons.

143

DISTANCE 2 miles (3.2km)

ALLOW 3 hours

START Arc de Triomf metro station

FINISH Ciutadella Vila Olímpica metro station

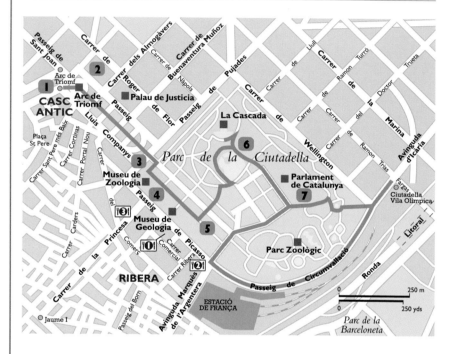

The Castell dels Tres Dragons (Castle of the Three Dragons), built by Lluís Domènech i Montaner as the café and restaurant for the 1888 Universal Exhibition, was Barcelona's first Moderniste building. Domènech i Montaner mobilized a team of glass workers, ceramicists, sculptors and carpenters to construct his workshop based on the British Arts and Crafts model. The building was named after a mid–19th-century comedy written by the father of Catalan theatre, Serafí Pitarra.

The exposed brickwork and visible iron supports were both architectural novelties at the time. Domènech i Montaner's building became a forum where Moderniste architects met to experiment with crafts and exchange ideas. The building is now host to Barcelona's Museu de Zoologia (Zoology Museum).

4 Continue down the west side of the park past the greenhouse, the geology museum and the Umbracle or Shaded Garden.

The Hivernacle (Greenhouse) is an interesting building with a café and restaurant, host to jazz concerts in summer. The Museu de Geologia was the city's first public museum, displaying rocks, minerals and fossils along with exhibits on Catalonia and Spain. The museum is next to the Umbracle, a shaded, 19th-century greenhouse for jungle plants that grow best in shade.

5 Cut across the park, past the lake, to La Cascada, the waterfall near the far corner.

This monumental, über-dramatic Josep Fontseré creation, presented as part of the 1888 Universal Exhibition, includes 'rocks' by a young architecture student named Antoni Gaudí. His first public work is appropriately natural and organic, and certainly a hint of things to come, though one wonders why he didn't just use... rocks. In fact, Gaudí's rocks, as would befit a young artist, are somewhat exaggeratedly rocky, overacting a trifle.

6 Walk through the park to the Parlament de Catalunya, the Catalan Parliament, significantly located in the middle of the military complex that oppressed Catalonia for so long.

Walking through the park, look for the well-marked Australian oaks, lindens, Canary palms, Corsican pines, blue palms, date palms, orange trees, magnolias, Australian pines, silk trees, Norwegian blacks, cypress trees and arbutus trees. There are also over 100 bird species resident in the park, including a large colony of grey herons. Sculptures by nearly every 19th- and 20th-century Catalan sculptor – Frederic Marès, Eusebi Arnau, Josep Clarà, Josep Llimona, Pau Gargallo, Manuel Fuxà and others – are scattered through the park, notably Josep Llimona's achingly forlorn *Desconsol (Desolation)*, a female nude in an attitude of despair placed in the reflecting pool in front of the Parliament building.

7 Walk through or past the zoo and out of the northeastern corner of the park to the Ciutadella-Vil.la Olímpica metro and tramway stop. Alternatively, walk out to Avinguda Marquès d'Argentera and continue around the Passeig de Circumval.lació.

ABOVE: A RESIDENT OF BARCELONA'S ZOO

ABOVE: *DESCONSOL* BY JOSEP LLIMONA, WITH THE PARLIAMENT OF CATALONIA BEHIND

WHERE TO EAT

⬛ PEIXATERIA LA PARADETA,
Carrer Comercial 7;
93-268-1939.
A fish and seafood store: choose
your fish and dine at long tables. €

⬛ DIONISIOS,
Av. Marquès de l'Argentera 27;
93-268-2472.
Greek and Mediterranean fare next
to the entrance to the Ciutadella
park. €€

⬛ SANTA MARIA,
Comerç 17;
93-315-1227.
Creative cuisine just a block from
the park. €€

Barcelona's superb zoo occupies the
entire bottom section of the Parc de la
Ciutadella. A well-equipped reptile house
and a full complement of African animals
attract mobs of visitors, while the dolphin
show generally performs to a capacity
crowd. The walk around the outside
of the wall provides nearly smelling
salts-strength zoo fragrances when the
wind is right, but the views into the
Estació de França partly compensate. The
Ciutadella-Vil.la Olímpica metro takes
you back to Plaça Urquinaona, next to
Plaça de Catalunya, while the tramway
T4 offers a pretty ride through much of
Barcelona's newest architecture out to the
Fòrum complex of Avinguda Diagonal.
www.zoobarcelona.com

Sarrià: Leafy upper Barcelona village

Once a country village, Sarrià is now a rural enclave overtaken by the urban sprawl, though its small-town character endures.

A thousand-year-old village that looked out over Barcelona from its perch in the beginnings of the Sierra de Collserola hills rising up behind the city, Sarrià was gradually outrun, though never overrun, by the expanding urban giant. A refuge for merchants, teachers, poets and artists, Sarrià became known as the city's premier school district as the summer mansions built by the city's textile barons were abandoned by subsequent generations either too numerous or too impecunious to maintain the grandeur of their forbears. The late poet J.V. Foix (1893-1987), published in Catalan in neighbouring France throughout the Franco regime, is a hero in Sarrià, where his descendants are still the owners of Sarrià's famous Foix pastry shops. Now almost completely pedestrianized, Sarrià retains its village charm at a distance of 4 miles (6.4km) from the Barcelona harbour, a mere 15 minutes by train. Its houses reflect an era when this village within a city was a flower-filled garden at the edge of the roaring metropolis.

From the Reina Elisenda metro stop climb up to Passeig de la Reina Elisenda de Montcada and turn left to the Mercat de Sarrià, a two-minute walk.

This redbrick neo-Mudéjar produce market is a small version of the Boqueria market downtown and a colourful place for a browse through the fish stalls and vegetable stands. Several little in-market bars provide good spots for a coffee and a sandwich, along with a look through the local newspapers for concerts or other cultural events around town. Exit the market through the back door directly across from the entrance and turn left for three steps and then make an immediate right into the tiny and flower-choked Plaça de Sant Gaietà, Sarrià's smallest square, presided over by Barcelona's biggest bougainvillea bush.

2 Go down Carrer Pare Miquel de Sarrià along the side of the market to Carrer Major de Sarrià and turn left uphill. Walk through Carrer de Graus, take a left on Carrer Avió Plus Ultra up to Carrer Margenat and then walk back down Major de Sarrià.

Directly across the street is a small *estanco*, a stamp shop with sandstone arches with the date 1564 carved into the stone, attesting that this is an early Sarrià structure left over from the village's agricultural past. Walking left up Major de Sarrià, the excellent Iskia wine store is on the corner of Carrer de Graus. The restaurant on your left with a lush garden is Vivanda.

WHERE TO EAT

|O| VIVANDA,
Major de Sarrià 134;
93-203-1918.
A good dining choice for polished and creative cuisine al fresco from May through October. €€

|O| TRAM-TRAM,
Major de Sarrià 121;
93-204-8518.
Haute cuisine in upper Barcelona by master chef Isidre Soler. €€€

|O| EL VELL SARRIÀ,
Major de Sarrià 93;
93-204-5710.
Specialists in rice dishes in a handsome 17th-century farmhouse. €€

3 Walk back to Carrer de l'Avió Plus Ultra and take a look at the wisteria-covered house across the corner, green in summer and purple when the wisteria is in full bloom. Walk up Carrer de l' Avió Plus Ultra.

The street is named for the airplane flown by El Generalísimo's brother Nicolás from the Azores to Argentina in 1934, making him the Spanish Lindbergh (ironically, since Nicolás Franco, known as 'the good Franco' was a Republican, whereas Charles Lindbergh was at one point enamoured of the German Third Reich). Walk to the end of Carrer Avió Plus Ultra, past the nonpareil Flora Miserachs flower store, to the end of the

DISTANCE 1 mile (1.6km)

ALLOW 2 hours

START Reina Elisenda metro station

FINISH Sarrià metro station

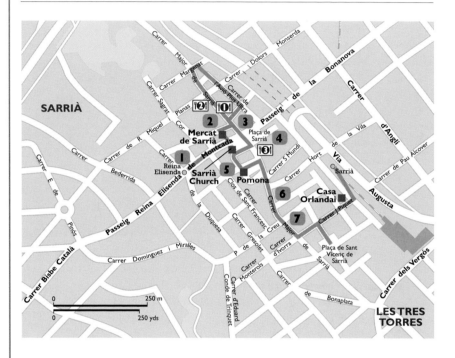

street, come back out and walk down past Tram-Tram at No. 121 and all the way back to Plaça de Sarrià.

4 Walk around Plaça de Sarrià, with a probe into Carrer Menor de Sarrià.

If Carrer Major is the biggest street in Sarrià, Carrer Menor is the smallest, with a total length of about a dozen paces. The houses on Carrer Menor de Sarrià and, especially, the house past the end of the street, are richly decorated with

sgraffito (see page 32) designs. Plaça de Sarrià holds antiques markets on alternate Thursdays and farm produce markets every other Saturday. Back across Reina Elisenda is the first of the two Foix pastry stores, with a bust of poet J.V. Foix inside to the right. The house next door, on the corner, is a handsome structure with a sundial. The church has been destroyed and rebuilt so often that it has only one interesting architectural element: the lovely ochre hexagonal stone bell tower that is beautifully illuminated at night.

ABOVE: POMONA, GODDESS OF THE HARVEST, BY JOSEP CLARÀ

5 Go through Placeta del Roser and left on Carrer Rector Volta into Plaça Consell de la Vila.

Placeta del Roser runs along the side of the Sarrià church into Carrer Rector Volta and into Consell de la Vila, home of the Sarrià town hall. The buxom bronze figure standing by the stairs into the Town Hall is Pomona, Goddess of the Harvest, by Josep Clarà (1878-1958), a longtime *sarrianenc* whose house and sculpture-filled garden is across Via Augusta on Carrer del Doctor Carulla. Pomona is a reference to Sarrià's history as a farming town and her exuberant splendour in front of the police station is a homage to Mediterranean earthiness and sensuality. Pomona's sisters (or other versions of herself) fill the Barcelona Town Hall in Plaça de Sant Jaume.

6 Walk out to Major de Sarrià and down five minutes to the corner of Carrer del Pedró de la Creu and the second Foix pastry shop.

On the left corner of Plaça Consell de la Vila and Major de Sarrià is the Vell Sarrià restaurant, a 17th-century farmhouse with lovely overhead beams that are little more than bark-stripped tree trunks. Moving down Major de Sarrià, don't miss the ivy-covered house at the corner of Carrer Canet, or the row of tiny workers' houses along the right side of the street, built by a textile baron for his employees. The Foix pastry store on the next corner has a plaque stating that the poet was born here, with one of his most famous

verses, beginning with the immortal 'Tot amor es latent en l'altre amor' (Every love is latent in the other love).

7 From the corner of Pedró de la Creu continue down a block to Bar Tomàs, on the corner of Carrer d'Ivorra. Turn left on Jaume Piquet across the street, turn right on Carrer de Cornet i Mas and walk down to Plaça de Sant Vicenç de Sarrià.

A left turn into Carrer de Jaume Piquet leads to Carrer Cornet i Mas and down into Plaça de Sant Vicenç de Sarrià, with Sarrià's patron saint on a pedestal and two more representations of the saint over the right uphill corner. Walk back up to Carrer Jaume Piquet, go right past the lovely wooden doorways at No. 21 and the Art Nouveau façade at No. 38 to the Casa Orlandai at the corner of Mare de Déu de Núria, a café and cultural centre in a Moderniste palace. The Sarrià metro stop just past Casa Orlandai connects to Plaça de Catalunya in 15 minutes.

153

OPPOSITE: PLAÇA SANT VICENÇ DE SARRIA; ABOVE: SARRIÀ DOOR KNOCKER

Lesser-known Gaudí and Residential chic

A walk that reveals two of Gaudí's finest treasures, the CosmoCaixa science museum and another Puig i Cadafalch Moderniste mansion.

Sant Gervasi is a hybrid of Eixample-like urban blocks in a leafy upper city outskirt. Contained by Via Augusta to the west and Carrer Balmes to the east, the area is primarily residential, though there are plenty of shops and services sprinkled throughout this traditionally upper middle class and, initially, aristocratic refuge. King Martí I l'Humà (1356-1410), called Martin the Humane for the advances in medicine achieved under his reign, built his summer palace at the top of Sant Gervasi on the site of Gaudí's Torre de Bellesguard. Half a millennium later, Barcelona's captains of industry built their handsome hillside mansions throughout the upper reaches of the neighbourhood. The CosmoCaixa Science Museum, two Gaudí creations, and other Moderniste buildings highlight Sant Gervasí's architectural treasures, while the boulevards swarm with schoolchildren and young professionals in the middle of what can often resemble a rolling street party.

1 From the Sarrià metro stop, cross Via Augusta and go down a block to the corner of Carrer del Doctor Carulla and turn left to the Josep Clarà library and sculpture garden at the third corner.

These mid-19th century Franco-era apartment buildings are notoriously ordinary, but the zone is considered one of Barcelona's most distinguished. The Josep Clarà public library and sculpture garden, with another series of bronze nudes, occupies the corner of Carrer Calatrava. For a small but fascinating detour, walk a block up Carrer Calatrava, turn left on Carrer Pau Alcover and cut immediately right up the Camí del Cementiri de Sarrià, a quiet cemetery filled with a jumble of sculptures and ornate Art Nouveau family tombs. A map of the cemetery is available at the main entrance. Look for the Gothic columns and angels at tomb 9 of area 1, and the pensive angel, finger touching lip, pondering The Meaning of It All, at tomb 10 of area 2.

2 Walk back down Carrer Calatrava two blocks to Carrer dels Vergós and turn left to the Mercat Tres Torres. Continue another street down and turn left into Carrer d'Alacant and Gaudí's Col.legi de les Teresianes.

Carrer Vergós between Carrer Calatrava and the Tres Torres market has several interesting small Moderniste houses, known in Catalonia as *torres* whether they have towers or not. The market on the corner is the smallest of all of Barcelona's

WHERE TO EAT

🍴 **EL PESCADITO DE MANDRI,**
Carrer Mandri 54;
93-418-8215.
Simple fare served at the bar or at tables at the back. €

🍴 **LA BALSA,**
Infanta Isabel 4;
93-211-5048.
A lush garden perch under canvas awnings serving fine Catalan fare. €€€

🍴 **EL ASADOR DE ARANDA,**
Av. Tibidabo 31;
93-417-0115.
Castilian roasts in a stunning Moderniste mansion. €€€

municipal semi-open-air markets, and far from the cheapest, though the produce is of high quality. The café inside the market is always a friendly and handy place to stop for a coffee or a *caña* (draught beer). Down from the market and to the left, Carrer d'Alacant passes the back of Gaudí's Col.legi de les Teresianes (School of the Company of Santa Teresa de Jesús).

3 Walk around the Teresiana school building and check at the security shack to see if there is any way you may be allowed to visit the interior, that day or any other.

Contracted in 1889 to finish a job begun by another architect, Gaudí was

DISTANCE **2.5 miles (4km)**

ALLOW **3 hours**

START **Sarrià metro station**

FINISH **Avinguda del Tibidabo metro station**

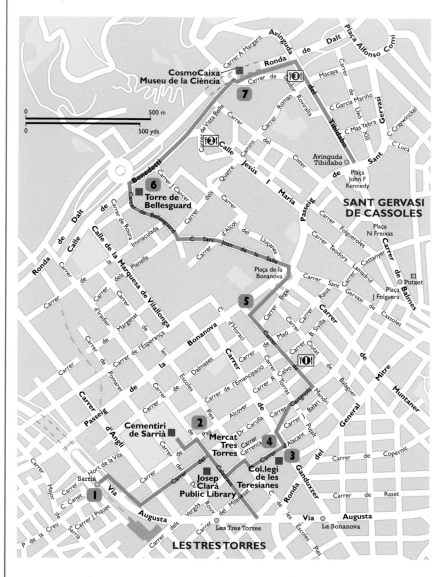

constrained by budget and by already standing construction in this project. Steep and narrow catenary arches and Mudéjar exposed brick pillars are the exterior themes, whereas inside on the second floor are two rows of fluid looping arches running across the width of the building. Brick columns are topped with T-shaped brick capitals (for St Theresa). Tiny garden courtyards reprise the Moorish patio tradition. The marble doorstep bears the famous *'todo se pasa'* (All things pass) quote by mystic writer and poet Santa Teresa de Avila (1515-82), even as the worn stone and lettering fades under the footsteps of 120 years of Teresiana schoolgirls.

COL.LEGI DE LES TERESIANES;

For visits TEL: 93/317-7652— or, from within Spain, 902-076-621 www.rutadelmodernisme.com

4 Hike up Carrer de Ganduxer, cutting right through Plaça de Ferran Casablancas and over another block to Carrer de Mandri, the main artery through Sant Gervasi.

Carrer Mandri is lined with shops, bars, restaurants, terraces and scores of young mothers pushing baby carriages. The far side of the street has most of the best taverns, including the excellent Pescadito de Mandri. At the end of Carrer de Mandri across Passeig de la Bonanova, take a look into the intimate Passatge de Güell, named for the family of Gaudí's great patron Eusebi Güell (1846-1918).

5 Walk to the right down Passeig de la Bonanova past the Lasalle school grounds to Plaça de la Bonanova, and left up Carrer Joan de la Salle to the intersection. Continue straight to Gaudí's Torre de Bellesguard at No. 20 Carrer de Bellesguard.

Built between 1900-09 over the ruins of the summer palace of the last Catalan-Aragonese sovereign Martí I l'Humà, this homage to King Martí is complete with Gothic crenellated battlements, towers, gargoyles, as well as Gaudí's catenary arches and mosaics of *trencadis* in stone and coloured ceramics. Constructed of the same earthy slate from the Collserola hills around and behind the site, Torre Bellesguard blends uncannily into the landscape. Stained-glass red and gold markings of the Catalan flag adorn the tower with Gaudí's four-armed Greek cross. Over the door is the inscription *sens*

ABOVE: THE TRAMVIA BLAU, THE LITTLE BLUE TROLLEY BUS UP TO THE TOP OF TIBIDABO

pecat fou concebuda (without sin was she conceived), referring to the Immaculate Conception of the Virgin Mary, while above is a colourful Bell Esguard (beautiful view). Benches with *trencadis* mosaics show dolphins bearing the four crimson bars of the Catalan flag and the Corona d'Aragó (Crown of Aragón), an allusion to Catalonia's medieval empire when it was said that 'not even a fish dared swim the Mediterranean without showing the colours of the Catalan flag.' A private residence, the colourful interior is rarely viewable, though photographic studies show a maze of catenary arches.

6 From Torre de Bellesguard, climb for two minutes to the Ronda de Dalt. Walk right for 10 minutes to the CosmoCaixa Museu de la Ciència.

ABOVE: COSMOCAIXA, INTERACTIVE SCIENCE MUSEUM

Make Wood Without Damaging the Forest, all linked with attempting to solve some of the major environmental problems of our time.

COSMOCAIXA;
Teodor Roviralta 55
TEL: 93/212—6050
www.cosmocaixa.com

7 From the CosmoCaixa, continue along the Ronda de Dalt to the corner of Avinguda del Tibidabo and turn right. Walk down past the Frare Blanc Moderniste mansion across the street from *The Shadow of the Wind's* Aldaya Palace at No. 32, and continue down to Plaça de John F. Kennedy and the Avinguda del Tibidabo metro station.

Avinguda del Tibidabo is rich in architecture, from the houses up above the Ronda all the way down to the Bonanova. At No. 31, the home of the Asador de Aranda restaurant, Casa Roviralta, is known as the Frare Blanc (White Friar) for the order of white habit-clad Dominican monks who once occupied a farmhouse-monastery here. Built by Moderniste architect Joan Rubió i Bellver in 1913, this massive structure of exposed brick and white surfaces faces the Carlos Ruiz Zafón novel *The Shadow of the Wind's* Aldaya Palace at No. 32 across the street, the mansion where the most dramatic moments of the story are played out. From here a five-minute walk will reach the Avinguda del Tibidabo metro station, and for connections to the top of Tibidabo, the Tramvia Blau (Blue Trolley) stop.

This superb interactive science museum just below Tibidabo is a boon for both young and old. Displays include the Geological Wall, a history of rock formations studied through a transversal cutaway; the Underwater Forest, showcasing species and climate of an Amazonian rainforest in a large greenhouse; sustainable exploitation tactics such as The Red Line: How to

Pedralbes to Camp Nou

A downhill hike through half a millennium of humanity, from early Gothic asceticism to Moderniste exuberance to contemporary sports glamour.

Pedralbes is where Barcelona's late 19th- and early 20th-century industrialists built their most elaborate mansions, a neighbourhood of gardens and palatial estates towering over the steamy urban tumult. The first aristocrat to take to the hills was Reina Elisenda de Montcada (1292-1364), widow of Catalan Count-King Jaume II el Just, who spent 37 years cloistered in the Mediterranean Gothic Monestir de Pedralbes, which she founded as a Clarist convent. As if drawn by Elisenda, the rest of Barcelona's bluebloods and magnates followed. Downhill from Pedralbes, a walk through the gardens and parks of lower Sarrià leads to the Pavellons Güell, the gatehouse of the Güell estate where the law school now stands. The Palau Reial de Pedralbes, originally built in the 1920s for King Alfonso XIII and now the home of the Museum of Decorative Arts, faces the western end of the Diagonal. Just downhill is the Futbol Club Barcelona complex, where a different kind of elite performs.

I From the Reina Elisenda metro stop walk to the right on Passeig de Reina Elisenda to the corner of Carrer Pere de Montcada and turn right up to Carrer del Monestir. Walk left for 10 minutes to Plaça del Monestir and the monastery of Pedralbes.

Crossing the viaduct over Avinguda de J.V. Foix, impressive post-Moderniste mansions are off to the left, one the home of the Creu Blanca (White Cross) clinic and the other the American Consulate. Up on Carrer del Monestir, the houses at Nos. 20 and 22 have lovely *sgraffito* (see page 32) designs. The circular square, Plaça de Jaume II, has a giant fig tree in the centre. The way down to the Plaça del Monestir is lined with spectacular houses, nearly all of which have been taken over by schools, clinics or institutes of one kind or another.

2 Walk around Plaça del Monestir and check out the superb estates on the square. Go inside the church, Santa Maria de Pedralbes, if it's open, before visiting the monastery.

Pedralbes was named for the white or at least light-coloured stones (from *petr*-stone, as in petrify and *albus*-white, as in albino), of which it was constructed in the 14th century. The church is related to Santa Maria del Mar, her country cousin, but lacking Santa Maria del Mar's spaciousness and streamlined upsweep. The tomb of Reina Elisenda on the right side of the nave shows the monastery's founder dressed as a queen; the other face

WHERE TO EAT

🍽️ EL MATÓ DE PEDRALBES,
Bisbe Català 10;
93-204-7962.
Simple country cooking across from the Monestir de Pedralbes. €€

🍽️ NEICHEL,
Beltrán i Rózpide 16 bis;
93-203-8408.
Artful Mediterranean cuisine in the hands of an Alsatian master near Pabellons Güell. €€€

🍽️ EL TRITON,
Carrer Alfambra 16;
93-203-3085.
Roast sea bass or goat in a classical setting just west of the Palau Reial. €€

of her tomb is visible from the inside, where Reina Elisenda is dressed as a nun of the Order of St Clare. The highlights of the inside of the monastery are the rare triple-tiered cloister and the Sant Miquel chapel painted in 1346 by Ferrer Bassa. Also on display are the nuns' day cells, dormitory, dining hall, kitchen, and chapterhouse.

3 Turn right coming out of the Monestir de Pedralbes and walk down the cobblestoned Baixada del Monestir, bearing left as you emerge down towards Carrer Bisbe Català.

The so-called *Conventet* (little convent) across the way, quarters for the Franciscan

OPPOSITE: TRIPLE-TIERED CLOISTER AT THE MONESTIR DE PEDRALBES

DISTANCE **3 miles (4.8km)**

ALLOW **3.5 hours**

START **Reina Elisenda metro station**

FINISH **Palau Reial metro and tramway station**

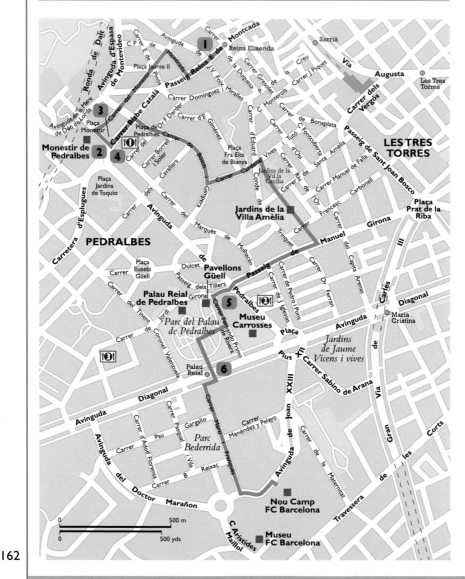

OPPOSITE: TOMB OF REINA ELISENDA IN THE PEDRALBES MONASTERY

monks who were required to celebrate Holy Communion (and who knows what else?) for the Clarist nuns across the street, is as architecturally interesting as the monastery, with *sgraffito* designs (see page 32), elaborate stone capitals carved by the Toulousain school of stoneworkers, and tall cypress trees. Across Carrer del Bisbe Català is a Moderniste building housing a bank and a pharmacy, and, next door, the Mató de Pedralbes restaurant.

4 **Walk left down Carrer del Bisbe Català and take a right on Carrer de Bosch i Gimpera, continue for 10 minutes past the Reial Club de Tenis, and go left into Carrer del Cardenal Vives i Tutó. Then cut through the gardens of Vil.la Cecília, continue through the gardens of Vil.la Amèlia to Passeig de Manuel Girona. Go right and cross Avinguda de Pedralbes until you reach the Pavellons Gaudí on the far corner.**

This part of the walk will take 20 to 30 minutes, but most of it goes through parks and gardens. The first 10 minutes traverse a modern complex of apartment buildings that, while much sought after as living accommodation, are of no architectural interest. At the corner of Vives i Tutó and Carrer del Trinquet is a lovely Moderniste house with an Art Nouveau gazebo in the garden. On your way through Vil.la Cecilia, the Sarrià *Casal* or cultural centre, a good place for a coffee, look for the bronze Ophelia floating face down in the pool near the exit. The next garden, Vil.la Amèlia, is more verdant and has a terrace café

with tables. Passeig Manuel de Girona leads to the right across Avinguda de Pedralbes to Gaudí's famous Finca Güell gatehouse, next to a wrought-iron gate decorated with Barcelona's only healthy dragon, an elaborate and fanciful beast with, for once, no sign of St George's lance slicing through him. Here, Gaudí was inspired not by the dragon of the St George legend but the dragon Ladon who guarded the Hesperides, daughters of Atlas, and their fabulous golden apple-bearing tree, a reference to national poet Jacint Verdaguer's epic poem *L'Atlántida*. This dragon, in chains, has outstretched claws that were once operated by a mechanism to open the gate, while his eyes burned red with inlaid glass. The ornamental letter G on the gate refers to the Güell family. The gatehouse is now Càtedra Gaudí, a Gaudí library and study centre, as well as a key Ruta del Modernisme point.

5 **Walk through tiny Carrer George R. Collins, named for an eminent Gaudí scholar from Boston, and then turn left down Carrer Fernando Primo de Rivera to the side entrance to the gardens of the Palau Reial de Pedralbes.**

The Palau Reial de Pedralbes stands on the site of an 18th-century house inherited by Count Eusebi Güell from his father, a retreat for country holidays in an area of farms and woodlands. When Güell died in 1918, the house and its park were given to the Spanish royal family, who had the building demolished and replaced it with the present palace. The

royal family used it as their quarters for the 1929 International Exhibition. Later, the Second Spanish Republic (1931–36) made the palace municipal property and established the decorative arts museum here. Today it houses both the Museu de les Arts Decoratives and the Museu de la Ceràmica, as well as the Textile and Clothing Museum. The collections include furniture and ornaments from the 15th through 20th centuries, and ceramics from all over Spain from the 12th century to the present, as well as clothing and textiles.

6 Walk across Avinguda Diagonal and walk for 10 minutes through Carrer Martí i Franquès to Camp Nou, home of the Futbol Club Barcelona.

Billed during the Franco era as 'Més qu'un club' (More than a club), hinting that 'El Barça' stood for Catalan national pride and the struggle to regain a national identity, the post-Franco Barça is, if anything, more *catalanista* then ever now that nationalism is legal. The stadium seats 98,000 people and fills to capacity for big games. The guided tour of the FC Barcelona museum and facilities includes the five-screen video showing the football club's most memorable goals, along with player biographies and displays chronicling the history of one of Europe's most colourful and glamorous soccer clubs. Backtrack uphill from FC Barcelona to the Avinguda Diagonal where you will find the Palau Reial metro and tramway stop.

PEDRALBES MONASTERY: SANT MIQUEL CHAPEL PAINTINGS BY FERRER BASSA

Diagonal Mar: New Barcelona

Barcelona's newest architecture begins at the Pompeu Fabra university and extends by tram to the Forum at the eastern end of the Diagonal.

The private Universitat Pompeu Fabra just north of the Ciutadella park contains some of Barcelona's best new architecture. Military barracks from the 19th century and the cistern that once stored the park's water supply have been ingeniously converted to a library, lecture halls, and study spaces. A short hop on the T4 tram, boarding at the Wellington stop, glides down its grassy track to the Rafael Moneo Auditori and the Teatre Nacional de Catalunya by Ricardo Bofill. After exploring these two glass, wood and steel structures, a walk through Plaça de les Glòries and the Mercat dels Encants Vells, the Barcelona flea market, ends only a block from Jean Nouvel's polychrome glass gherkin, Torre Agbar, looming like an iridescent rocket ship over Plaça de les Glòries. Again boarding the tramway at the Ca l'Aranyó station, a 15-minute ride east along Avinguda Diagonal passes through the new Diagonal Mar district of residential buildings to the Fòrum complex of concert venues, bathing areas, and exhibition halls.

1 From the Ciutadella Vila Olímpica tramway stop, walk up to Carrer de Ramon Trias Fargas to the entrance into the Pompeu Fabra university. Walk through the underground passage between the main building and the library reading room before finding your way out to the Wellington stop on the T4 tram line.

The Universitat Pompeu Fabra's main building occupies the barracks that once housed the armies of Felipe V after the siege and conquest of Barcelona in 1714. The lecture hall building has been completely glassed in, while the study rooms for researchers are behind a wooden façade. A walk through the downstairs section of the library leads through to a curious trompe l'oeil passageway in which leaning lateral beams and supports suggest a rising ramp which, in fact, is dead level, causing a tendency in the walker to lean and lurch. Once the cistern for the Ciutadella waterfall built in 1880 by Josep Fontseré, the Dipòsit de les Aigües was converted to a library in 1999 by contemporary architects Lluís Clotet and Ignacio Paricio. Massive, 3ft-(1m)-thick walls, perforated and crowned with mid-point arches, surround reading stalls and stacks.

2 Duck out into Carrer Ramon Trias Fargas and walk up a block and out to the Wellington tramway stop for a five-minute ride up to the Auditori i Teatre Nacional stop on Avinguda Meridiana just a short walk from some of Barcelona's newest architecture.

Rafael Moneo's wood-panelled Auditori at Carrer Lepant 150 has frequently been described as inside-of-a-guitar-like with its sleek wood-lined main concert hall a nearly perfect aesthetic antonym of the Art Nouveau Palau de la Música Catalana. The building opened in 1999 at the intersection of the city's three widest and longest avenues (Diagonal, Gran Via, and Meridiana) near Plaça de les Glòries Catalanes, the transport hub of the Barcelona of the future, with the high speed AVE train station and the city spreading out to the east through Diagonal Mar and the Fòrum. The Auditori has three concert halls, of which the 2,200 capacity Pau Casals is the largest.
www.auditori.com

3 Walk east across Carrer de Padilla into Plaça de les Arts and up the stairway of the Teatre Nacional de Catalunya.

Ricardo Bofill's post-neoclassical Teatre Nacional, built between 1991 and 1996, has been compared to a glass-enclosed Parthenon, with massive Doric columns and, for Barcelona, an extraordinarily balanced and rational layout. The main venue has a 900-spectator capacity, while the acoustics, stage management technology, and even the form and quality of the seats have been elaborately planned to maximize all aspects of theatre and dance productions.
www.tnc.cat
For guided tour reservations:
TEL: 93/306-5749 or visites@tnc.cat

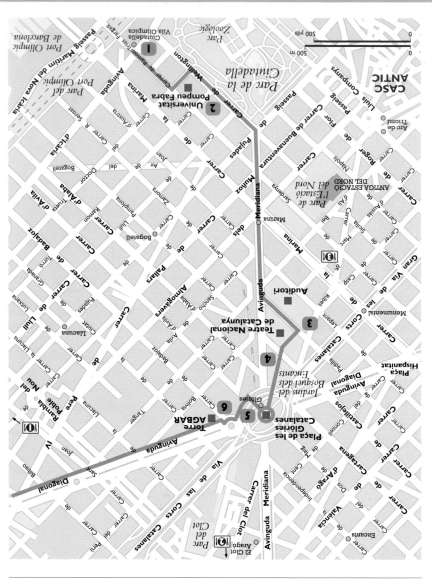

DISTANCE 8 miles (12.8km)

ALLOW 4 hours

START Ciutadella-Vil.la Olímpica tramway station

FINISH Avinguda Diagonal

WHERE TO EAT

ELS PESCADORS,
Plaça Prim 1;
93-225-2018.
Rice and seafood in a pretty square in
Poble Nou. €€

HERMANOS TOMAS,
Pare Pérez del Pulgar 1;
93-345-7148.
Game and authentic Catalan cooking
in eastern Barcelona. €€

PIRATAS,
Ausias Marc 157;
93-245-7642.
Foie gras, cheeses, caviars and fine
wines in a tiny tavern two blocks
from the Auditori. €€€

4 Walk around the Auditori and
through the park across Carrer de
Castillejos into Jardins del Bosquet dels
Encants and cross to the Plaça de les
Glòries Catalanes.

Barcelona's flea market, a wonderful
hodge-podge of stolen, found, recycled,
and otherwise miscellaneous bric-a-brac,
still rages here at the epicentre of the new
Barcelona of shopping malls, arts venues
and skyscrapers sprouting up around it.
Functioning from Wednesday through
Saturday, Els Encants ('The Enchantments)
suggests, in its name, magic, and there
has always been a magical quality in
the curios and whimsical objects and
coincidences that seem to materialize

here. A definite gypsy flavour still
permeates Els Encants, while the little
bars and taverns around the edges of the
market serve simple sustenance unfazed
by molecular gastronomy and, for that
matter, the 21st century.

5 Now walk back through the Plaça
de les Glòries Catalanes to the
burly skyscraper across the way.

Jean Nouvel's Torre Agbar is a dead
ringer for Sir Norman Foster's St Mary
Axe tower (disrespectfully referred to
as the Gherkin) on London's South
Bank, opened in June 2005. Described
as 'a geyser under permanent calculated
pressure' by the architect, the tower
is covered by 56,619 translucent and
transparent panels in 25 different colours,
along with 4,400 windows. The louvred
panels tilt to deflect the sun, so the
surface appears to be in constant flux.
www.torreagbar.com

6 Walk east past the corner of Carrer
Ciutat de Granada to the Ca
l'Aranyó tramway stop on Avinguda
Diagonal. Catch the next tram to the
Fòrum at the east end of the Diagonal.

Much of the development on either
side of this section of the Diagonal
was constructed in the build-up to
the celebration of the 2004 Fòrum de
les Cultures. Originally hailed as the
successor to the three major international
events ('The Universal Exposition of
1888, the International Exhibition of
1929, and the Olympic Games of 1992)

that Barcelona used to catapult itself to greater world stature and commercial grandeur, this event was not so successful. World events conspired to hijack the global stage, and the Forum largely fizzled, with opposition from all quarters of the political spectrum and criticism over real estate speculation, eviction of communities of gypsies, high admission prices, and no-shows by key featured lecturers. What remains is the Herzog & de Meuron Fòrum building, several not frequently booked concert venues, a rocky bathing area that few *barcelonins* have shown much interest in using, and an aquarium that initially struggled to meet EU environmental regulations. Nevertheless, as Barcelona's population

grows and moves further east (the only direction it *can* move in) and Plaça de les Glòries Catalanes becomes the city centre that Plaça Catalunya has been since the early 20th century, the Fòrum may take its place as successor to the Roman forum in Plaça Sant Jaume 2000 years ago. With Jean Nouvel's phallic Torre Agbar at one end of the new Barcelona and the delta of Venus-like Fòrum building at the other, Diagonal Mar seems positioned to generate excitement. Until now, this cold and remote end of town has lacked the verve to compete with the high-speed, high-energy Barcelona of today. The T4 tramway or the L4 metro line just up Rambla de Prim are 15 minutes from the city centre.

INDEX

ACKNOWLEDGEMENTS

The Automobile Association would like to thank the following photographers, companies and picture libraries for their assistance in the preparation of this book.

Abbreviations for the picture credits are as follows – (AA) AA World Travel Library.

Front cover: AA/P Wilson; 3 AA/M Chaplow; 7 AA/P Wilson; 8 © Jon Arnold Images Ltd/Alamy; 13 © 4Corners Images/ SIME/Fantuz Olimpio; 14 AA/S McBride; 15 AA/S McBride; 17 © Ramon Manent/CORBIS; 19 AA/M Chaplow; 20 AA/M Jourdan; 21 AA/S McBride; 24/5 AA/M Jourdan; 26/7 AA/S Day; 28 AA/M Jourdan; 31 AA/M Jourdan; 33 AA/S Day; 34/5 AA/S Day; 36 AA/S Day; 39 AA/S Day; 40 AA/M Jourdan; 42 AA/M Chaplow; 43 AA/C Sawyer; 45 AA/P Wilson; 48/9 AA/M Jourdan; 50 AA/P Wilson; 53 AA/P Wilson; 54 AA/S McBride; 55 AA/S McBride; 56/7 AA/M Chaplow; 58 AA/P Wilson; 61 © Mark Baynes/Alamy; 62 © Mark Baynes/Alamy; 64 AA/M Chaplow; 67 AA/M Chaplow; 68/9 World Pictures/Photoshot; 70 AA/S Day; 73 AA/M Chaplow; 74 AA/M Chaplow; 76 © Oso Media/Alamy; 79 © Oso Media/ Alamy; 81 © Neil Setchfield/Alamy; 82/3 AA/M Chaplow; 84 © Chris Hellier/Corbis; 85 © Ramon Manent/CORBIS; 87 AA/M Jourdan; 89 © David Taylor Photography/Alamy; 90/1 AA/S Day; 92 AA/M Jourdan; 95 AA/S Day; 96 AA/M Jourdan/ © Foundation Antoni Tapies, Barcelone/VEGAP, Madrid and DACS, London 2008; 97 AA/M Chaplow; 98/9 AA/S Day; 100 AA/S Day; 102 World Pictures/Photoshot; 104 AA/M Jourdan; 105 AA/S Day; 106/7 AA/M Chaplow; 108 AA/S McBride; 109 AA/S McBride; 111 © Sandra Baker/Alamy; 113 AA/M Chaplow; 114 AA/S Day; 115 AA/M Jourdan; 117 PhotoShot; 118 © Vincent Lowe/Alamy; 120 AA/S Day; 123 AA/M Jourdan; 124 AA/M Jourdan; 126/7 AA/S Day; 128 © Rough Guides/Alamy; 129 AA/M Jourdan; 132 AA/S Day; 133 AA/M Chaplow; 134 AA/M Jourdan/ © Succession Miro/ ADAGP, Paris and DACS, London 2008; 137 AA/S Day; 139 AA/M Jourdan; 140/1 AA/M Jourdan; 142 AA/S Day; 143 Mel Longhurst/World Illustrated/Photoshot; 145 AA/M Jourdan; 146/7 AA/S Day; 148 Marc Oromi; 151 Marc Oromi; 152 Marc Oromi; 153 Marc Oromi; 154 CosmoCaixa Barcelona, Ronald Stallard; 157 © Gregory Wrona /Alamy; 158/9 CosmoCaixa Barcelona, Ronald Stallard; 160 AA/S Day; 163 AA/M Jourdan; 165 AA/S Day; 166/7 AA/M Jourdan; 168 © Eastland Photo/Alamy; 171 © Turisme de Barcelona/Espai d'Imatge; 173 © Bob Masters/Alamy.

Every effort has been made to trace the copyright holders, and we apologize in advance for any accidental errors. We would be happy to apply the corrections in the following edition of this publication.